OVERCOMING TOO-BIG-TO-FAIL

A REGULATORY FRAMEWORK TO LIMIT MORAL HAZARD AND FREE RIDING IN THE FINANCIAL SECTOR

REPORT OF THE CEPS-ASSONIME TASK FORCE ON BANK CRISIS RESOLUTION

JACOPO CARMASSI, ELISABETTA LUCHETTI
AND STEFANO MICOSSI

WITH CONTRIBUTIONS FROM
DANIEL GROS AND KAREL LANNOO

WITH FINANCIAL SUPPORT OF UNICREDIT GROUP

D1521021

CENTRE FOR EUROPEAN POLICY STUDIES
BRUSSELS

This report is based on discussions in a Task Force on Bank Crisis Resolution, which was formed jointly by the Centre for European Policy Studies (CEPS), an independent policy research institute in Brussels, and Assonime, the Association of Joint Stock Companies incorporated in Italy. The members of the Task Force met three times between July 2009 and January 2010. A full list of members and invited guests and speakers can be found at the end of the report.

Acknowledgements: The authors wish to thank for useful observations and suggestions Marcello Bianchi, Margherita Bianchini, Edward Bowles, Charles Case, Luc Delvaux, Carmine Di Noia, Achim Dübel, Andrea Enria, Eva Hüpkes, Rosa Lastra, Sergio Lugaresi, Rainer Masera, Barbara Matthews, Maria Nieto, Luciano Panzani, Jean-Luc Vallens and the participants in the Task Force meetings. They maintain sole responsibility for the content of the report, which does not necessarily reflect the views of each individual bank or Task Force member.

Cover photo by Martin St-Amant

Centre for European Policy Studies
Place du Congrès 1, B-1000 Brussels
Tel: (32.2) 229.39.11 Fax: (32.2) 219.41.51
E-mail: info@ceps.eu
Website: http://www.ceps.eu

CONTENTS

List of Tables

List of Figures

List of Boxes

PREFACE

This report comes at crucial time. The acute crisis in financial markets seems to have passed and the authorities can switch their attention from the overriding task of avoiding a meltdown to more strategic considerations. The crisis has shown that the chaotic failure of large complex financial institutions can have very large costs. As this report argues convincingly, this implies that it will remain impossible to restore market discipline until some way can be found to allow even large institutions to fail in a less costly manner.

Following the chaos that followed the bankruptcy of Lehman Brothers, some have argued that the only solution is to break up all large financial institutions and that their risk-taking activities must be limited by law. Such actions are by no means necessary, however, and they may be hard to implement in practice and could entail large costs in terms of the availability of credit to the economy (e.g. if they reduced the ability of banks to hedge their credit positions). This report shows that alternative solutions exist that can achieve a more stable and resilient financial system without renouncing the benefits of multi-purpose financial institutions and innovative finance. These are predicated on effectively curtailing moral hazard and strengthening market discipline on banks' shareholders and managers by raising the cost of the banking charter to fully reflect its benefits for the banks, and restoring the possibility that all or at least most financial institutions could go bust, without triggering unmanageable systemic repercussions.

This report concentrates on how these issues can be dealt with in Europe where the cross-border aspects are abundantly in evidence. The quality of the report is due not only to the very detailed analysis of the authors, but also to the quality of the participants in this joint CEPS-Assonime Task Force, which received financial support from Unicredit and was composed of experts from large banks (and financial institutions), regulatory agencies and international organisations, bankruptcy judges and academics.

Daniel Gros
CEPS, March 2010

SUMMARY OF RECOMMENDATIONS

All EU cross-border banking groups would be required to sign up to a new deposit guarantee scheme managed by the European Banking Authority (EBA). The scheme would be fully funded ex-ante by levying fees determined on an actuarial risk basis. Participating banks would undertake to provide all relevant information required for effective supervision to the EBA and the Colleges of supervisors.

All banking groups would be supervised and, in case of need, subjected to mandatory resolution procedures on a consolidated basis, under the law of the parent company. Subsidiaries chartered in separate jurisdictions, but unable to survive a crisis of the parent company on their own, would also fall under the same authority.

Banking groups would be free to set up fully stand-alone subsidiaries, under the law of the host countries, but the entities would then have to meet precise requirements of independence of capital, liquidity and other critical functions.

All national supervisors would have administrative powers to manage early corrective action and resolution, according to the principles outlined by the Basel Supervisors.

Supervision, early action and reorganisation would be managed by strengthened Colleges of supervisors, under the leadership of the parent company supervisor and a regime of full exchange of information amongst interested national supervisors. The Colleges of supervisors would make their proposals to the EBA, which would sanction them with its own decisions and would mediate disputes between national supervisors.

By offering all interested parties in a resolution procedure the full guarantee that they will be heard and treated fairly before an independent authority, the EBA would create the conditions in which jurisdictions other than that of the parent company will be ready to accept delegating to the latter the resolution of the entire banking group on a consolidated basis. Mandated action will also ensure that supervisory forbearance would not be used to favour national interests to the detriment of stakeholders from other jurisdictions.

1. INTRODUCTION

As the financial crisis subsides, the new regulatory structure for the financial system is starting to take shape, with a number of legislative proposals already tabled, and even approved, in the United States, the European Union and the United Kingdom – the latter of which is once again showing its readiness to act unilaterally without consulting its EU partners. What is striking about these developments is not only that responses are not coordinated between the main financial centres, but that new rules are proposed and enacted without a common understanding of the nature and causes of the financial crisis, raising the risk of excessive and inconsistent regulation.

For instance, while most analysts would agree that credit-rating agencies should be stripped of their public franchise granted by US legislation, under whose cover they sold misleading ratings in the interest of issuers of toxic assets, the EU authorities have introduced similar legislation in the EU. Similarly, while there is little evidence that hedge funds contributed to the financial crisis in any manner, the idea that they should be subject to regulation, and even prudential supervision like banks, has political support.

Most importantly, a lack of understanding of the causes and dynamics of the financial crisis is leading legislators to create a regulatory structure for large banks and other financial institutions that is based on misleading concepts of systemic risk and systemic instability and is likely to augment moral hazard and the potential liabilities for taxpayers in countries hosting large financial centres.

Two fundamental truths should be recognised in this regard. First, herd behaviour by financial intermediaries and investors near the peak of a speculative bubble, both in the climb and the ensuing precipitous fall, wasn't a haphazard phenomenon due to uncontrollable psychological reasons. Rather, it was the result of destabilising monetary policy regimes in the leading financial centres – notably owing to the US Federal Reserve systematically intervening to prop up asset prices but never to counter their rise (Taylor, 2009; Carmassi et al., 2009).[1] To the extent that herd behaviour is due to destabilising monetary policy, building anti-cyclical brakes into banks' regulatory capital[2] will not eliminate instability as long as monetary policy rules aren't rectified.

Second, the fact that increasingly large, complex and interconnected financial institutions almost brought down the entire world financial system does not lead automatically to the conclusion that a new layer of regulation specifically addressing these financial institutions is required – a suggestion first advocated by the Group of Thirty (2009) that has subsequently found widespread support. For one thing, this approach would implicitly accept that the sources of systemic instability cannot be brought down to at least manageable proportions, and must therefore be accepted as a permanent feature of the financial system. This is by no means a warranted conclusion.

Explosive growth of financial intermediation was encouraged in the first place by asset inflation, which created opportunities for enormous gains from trading and speculative asset market positions. Within that context, institutional incentives were encouraging financial organisations to take reckless risks. The priority in regulatory reform should be to correct these distorted incentives, rather than forcing structural reorganisations and legal constraints on activities that may damage the efficiency of the financial system and hinder its ability to serve the credit needs of the economy.

Back to basics, the explosive growth in financial intermediation (Figure 1.1) was fuelled by a massive increase in borrowing – leading to unsustainable leverage – which in turn was instrumental in a massive increase in open positions in high-risk securities of uncertain liquidity promising disproportionate gains. Much of the increase in financial

---

[1] Similarly, in the events leading to the Great Wall Street Crash of 1929, (the promise of) lax monetary policy was embedded in the gold standard monetary regime. On this, see Galbraith (1954) and Kindleberger & Aliber (2005).

[2] As advocated by the so-called 'Geneva Report' of the International Centre for Monetary and Banking Studies (Brunnermeier et al., 2009).

intermediation took place within the financial sector itself (FSA, 2009a). The main source of funds for these asset market positions was the wholesale interbank market where large cross-border banks were the residual suppliers of liquidity for all the other players in the game (see Gorton & Metrick, 2009; Tucker, 2010). In practice, these banks were using their deposit base to multiply funds for speculation and generate a gigantic inverted pyramid of securities made up of other securities and yet again other securities. When asset prices started to fall, the house of cards fell back onto the banks, calling into question their ability to meet their obligations towards depositors and the very confidence in money. Without the money-multiplying capacity of the banks, the asset price bubble and the explosion of financial intermediation and aggregate leverage wouldn't have been possible.

Figure 1.1 Growth of banks' total assets, 2000-07 (2000=100)*

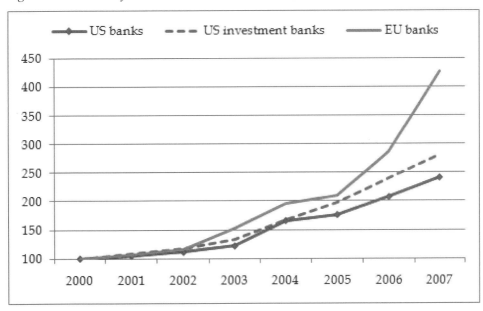

* US banks include Bank of America, Citigroup and JPMorgan Chase. US investment banks include Bear Stearns, Goldman Sachs, Lehman Brothers, Merrill Lynch and Morgan Stanley. EU banks include BNP Paribas, Deutsche Bank, Royal Bank of Scotland and UBS.

Source: Own calculations based on annual reports.

The rapid growth of financial intermediation and risk exposures was driven by dramatic increases in profitability. The Economist estimated that in 2007 the financial sector represented some 10% of value added in the US economy, but some 40% of its profits. Alessandri & Haldane (2009) have shown that, after remaining stable at around 5-7% for several decades, the return on equity of large UK banks tripled during the past three decades. The promise of ever-larger profits thus led to a major diversion of resources from productive investment to speculation in financial markets.

As one would expect, higher returns on equity were associated with higher return variability, indicating a sharply higher propensity to take risks (Figure 1.2). It appears that many financial institutions were behaving like 'plungers', rather than 'diversifiers', in James Tobin's classical terminology (Tobin, 1958): they were using all the levers of financial technology to achieve the largest possible return regardless of risk.

Figure 1.2 Return on equity for UK banks

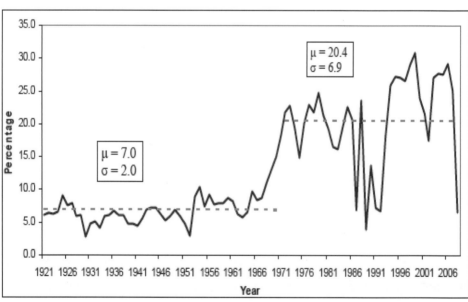

Source: Alessandri & Haldane (2009).

In turn, increasing returns were in the main achieved by leveraging own capital to unprecedented heights, increasing the share of proprietary assets in trading books, and taking bets on increasingly risky assets. As has been shown, these strategies have the effect of raising the sensitivity of banks' return on equity to aggregate market risk – in financial parlance, their β coefficient. Thus, what was trumpeted as shrewd management leading to higher institution-specific (α) returns, increasingly amounted to banks becoming exposed to similar risks, thus enhancing their exposure to common aggregate shocks (Alessandri and Haldane 2009).[3]

Such widespread use of extreme investment strategies by bankers indicates the presence of incentives affecting all banks, that is, the moral hazard created by the expectation that large banks will always be bailed out, owing to the feared consequences of their failure on overall financial stability. The downside in bankers' risk–return matrices was effectively truncated by public protections designed to preserve confidence in money and the banking system, which de facto entailed that banks could not fail. The events of the past two years have only aggravated the problem since the mishandled failure of Lehman Brothers convinced even more policy-makers and regulators that large financial institutions cannot be allowed to fail, effectively removing market discipline from large chunks of financial markets.

Thus, the debate on regulatory reform has been misled into concluding that there is no alternative to breaking up large financial institutions or limiting by law their risk-taking activities, as influentially advocated by Paul Volcker, former Chairman of the Federal Reserve and currently Chairman of the Economic Recovery Advisory Board under President Barack Obama.[4] However, this may be hard to do in practice[5] and

---

[3] As explained by Borio (2003), monitoring the financial system's exposure to aggregate shocks is precisely the main intended task for the new macro-prudential supervision that all the main regulatory systems are embracing as a panacea against a repetition of the horrendous events of 2008. Of course collecting the information can do no harm: but it does not explain, nor remove, the reasons why so many sophisticated bankers had earnestly pursued strategies that proved eventually to be so destructive for their organisations and their personal fortunes.

[4] See G-30 (2009), Recommendation 1b, pp. 27-28, and Volcker (2010).

[5] On this see Martin Wolf, "Why narrow banking alone is not the finance solution", *Financial Times*, 29 September 2008, and "Volcker's axe is not enough to cut the banks down to size", *Financial Times,* 27 January 2010. As has been argued, to an important extent risks were taken by banks indirectly, by financing positions formally in the books of other intermediaries through the interbank market.

could entail large costs for the availability of credit to the economy (e.g. if it reduced the ability of banks to hedge their credit positions).

We believe that such measures are by no means necessary: alternative solutions exist that can achieve a more stable financial system without renouncing the benefits of multi-purpose financial institutions and innovative finance. They are predicated on effectively curtailing moral hazard and strengthening market discipline on banks' shareholders and managers by raising the cost of the banking charter to fully reflect its benefits for the banks, and restoring the possibility to go bust for all, or at least most financial institutions, without unmanageable systemic repercussions. The new incentive structure for bankers should suffice to bring bloated finance back to normal proportions, relative to underlying economic activity, and make the financial system less exposed to systemic shocks.[6]

The new regulatory architecture must correct an obvious pitfall in banking regulation, that is, reliance on capital requirements based on risk-weighted assets. This approach is flawed since asset risk cannot be assessed and measured independently of market conditions and market sentiment (Brunnermeier et al., 2009; Kay, 2009). As a result, the need for capital will always be underestimated under favourable market conditions, leading to balance-sheet fragility and precipitous asset sales when market sentiment turns around.[7] Empirical evidence has confirmed that many financial

---

Therefore, placing constraints on banks' securities positions may not be sufficient to impede reckless risk-taking; on the other hand, the legal restrictions required to eschew all unwanted risk-taking may cripple the banks' ability to operate also in their normal commercial lending business.

[6] There would also be less need to regulate non-bank financial institutions, such as (pure) investment banks and private pools of capital (Di Noia & Micossi, 2009). Insurance companies should be restrained by the general rules of insurance, which require that all risks should be covered by adequate reserves determined from the probability distribution of adverse events. Writing up indefinite amounts of credit default swaps (CDS) on unknown risks, as AIG managed to do through its Financial Product division (AIGFP), should be illegal under general insurance regulation, without creating another domain of prudential regulation.

[7] "In an uncertain world values will also be uncertain, and the margins of uncertainty are very wide. The measurement of capital is not, and will never be, simultaneously exact or objective, and economically meaningful. The risk

institutions that got in trouble had shown comfortable regulatory capital (IMF, 2009).

However, we are not ready to recommend that capital requirements be scrapped altogether, as advocated by Kay (2009). A capital buffer is needed because massive asymmetries of information between bank managers, on the one side, and investors and regulators on the other, make it easy for bankers to accumulate excessive risks, in the quest for higher returns, before markets become aware. The dependency of large banks on wholesale markets, where 'runs' may happen even where retail deposits are well protected, confirms the limitations of risk-based capital and the need to refer to total leverage.[8] By limiting maturity transformation, regulatory capital places an automatic ceiling on risk-taking; monitoring capital in relation to total exposure reduces the need for close monitoring of the quality of banking assets.[9] Thus, capital requirements should be set in straight proportion to total assets or liabilities of banking groups.[10]

---

associated with a given portfolio of assets is only loosely related to the aggregate value of the assets … And it is a basic principle of risk analysis that the aggregate risk of a portfolio cannot be measured by adding up the risks of individual elements." Kay (2009, p. 8). Building anti-cyclical capital buffers may at best attenuate, but will not resolve the problem: any regulatory definition of capital allowances for risk is bound to create profitable opportunities for circumventing the rule.

[8] This aspect was called to our attention by Maria Nieto.

[9] A separate question that goes beyond the scope of this report is whether regulatory capital requirements should also be imposed on non-bank financial institutions, as such not enjoying the banking charter benefits. A prudent answer, taking into account the lessons from the recent crisis, is that any institution raising funds from the money market to invest in capital market securities, hence undertaking significant maturity transformation, should be required to hold a minimum regulatory capital, as a backstop against the potential shocks generated by its losses for the lenders of its liquidity.

[10] The Basel Committee on Banking Supervision has already envisaged the introduction of a leverage ratio unadjusted for risk, but as a complement rather than a substitute of risk-adjusted capital requirements (BCBS, 2009a). There is also a need to simplify and harmonise the definitions of capital across jurisdictions, notably by restricting regulatory capital to cash and equity and scrapping the more exotic components of dubious value in case of crisis (Di Noia & Micossi, 2009).

Fixing flaws in prudential capital rules does not remove moral hazard from the banking system, whose specific sources must be tackled separately, as will be discussed in the ensuing chapters. These are: a) the deposit-institution franchise, b) the implicit or explicit promise of bailout in case of threatened failure and c) regulatory forbearance.

The problem associated with the deposit franchise is well known (Rochet, 2008). Banks collect funds by offering to redeem deposits at par on demand; and make money by deploying the funds thus obtained in loans and investments with longer maturity; and keep (uncertain) capital to meet deposit redemptions. As long as depositors feel safe, they will not seek redemption of their deposits, but if they have doubts on the bank's solvency, they will all run for the exit, forcing rapid liquidation of banks' assets, possibly with large losses. A run on one bank may easily spread to other banks and endanger overall financial stability, as all banks scramble to recuperate liquidity by selling assets and calling back their credit lines in the interbank market.[11]

Deposit insurance can be effective in calming depositors' fears, but it also mutes their incentive to monitor the management of their banks, since they no longer risk losing their money. More importantly, deposit insurance has evolved in most countries into a system effectively protecting the bank, or the entire banking group, rather than the depositors: when a bank risks becoming insolvent, rather than simply letting it fail and pay its depositors, supervisors often step in to cover its losses and replenish its capital so as to avoid any adverse repercussions on market confidence. Moreover, most deposit insurance systems are inadequately funded by

---

[11] For an illuminating description of the contagion mechanisms that almost brought down world banking following Lehman's failure in September 2008, see Freixas (2009). Tucker (2010) examines the various ways in which banks used instruments such as money market mutual funds, asset-backed commercial paper and off-balance sheet vehicles to apparently increase liquidity by off-loading loans and securities and reducing maturity mismatches in their balance sheets – which came back to haunt them when the markets for these instruments became illiquid. By booking activities outside their balance sheets, banks were creating 'shadow banks', which were not subject to banking prudential rules. The effectiveness of banking regulation is obviously predicated on the ability to prevent non-bank financial institutions from acting like banks – notably by promising redemption of their liabilities on demand and at par – without a banking charter.

insured institutions, entailing an implicit promise that taxpayers' money will make up the difference, notably when confronting failure of a large bank.

Therefore, offering deposit accounts generates the very important benefit, for the bank or banking group, that markets and ordinary people are led to believe that the organisation as a whole is safe. As a result, they are more inclined to do business with that organisation and take greater risks than would otherwise be prudent. The bank, thus, will feel less pressure to hold adequate reserves and will be encouraged to tap its liquidity and capital buffers to raise returns. Therefore, its deposit base – while a source of stable funding – creates the occasion and the incentives for the bank to overextend and take excessive risks.

In sum, while financial stability is indeed much strengthened by deposit insurance, existing schemes must go back to their origin and cover only depositors, and never again other creditors, shareholders or the bank itself; no bail-out or recapitalisation of banks should be allowed under deposit guarantee schemes. The incentive for all stakeholders to monitor closely management strategies and risk-taking in their bank would be very much strengthened.

A related aspect in re-establishing a proper price for the banking charter is that banks should carry ex-ante the full cost of deposit protection, determined so as to make sure that in most circumstances the guarantee fund would be adequate to reimburse depositors when individual banks fail. Of course, no fund could ever be sufficient to meet a general banking crisis; but a fund of an appropriate size would offer adequate protection in normal circumstances, with only a predictable share of banks going bankrupt. This would be sufficient to bring about a more stable and resilient banking system where the likelihood of a systemic crisis would be smaller, since each bank would be less prone to excessive risk-taking.

Individual banks' fees for the deposit guarantee should be determined on the basis of a careful probabilistic assessment of the likelihood of failure within the overall pool of deposits and risks of the banking system (within appropriately defined market jurisdictions). This is where the risk profile of banks' asset and loan portfolios can be taken fully into consideration, together with, more broadly, the quality of bank management and risk control, thus creating effective penalties for riskier behaviour. Appropriate weights could also be applied to excessive reliance on less stable sources of finance, such as the wholesale money market, doubtful liquidity of investments, or opaque and complex legal structures. Size itself could be appropriately penalized by higher fees that would incorporate a probabilistic price for the potential threat for systemic stability. [12]

The second pillar required in order to greatly limit moral hazard in the financial system is removing credibly the promise that some financial institutions cannot fail. To this end, all main jurisdictions should establish special resolution procedures applicable to banks and banking groups, managed by an administrative authority, capable of tackling a bank crisis by acting early to correct emerging capital weaknesses, intervening decisively in promoting required reorganisations and, once all this failed, liquidating the bank with only limited systemic repercussions. Crisis prevention, reorganisation and liquidation would all be part of a unified resolution procedure managed for each bank or banking group in every country by an administrative authority with adequate powers, as will be described.[13]

In order to make resolution feasible, all banks and banking groups would be required to prepare and provide to their supervisors a document detailing the claims on the bank and their order of priority, the full consolidated structure of legal entities that depend on the parent company for their survival, and may therefore produce liabilities for the parent company, and a clear description of operational – as distinct from legal – responsibilities and decision-making, notably regarding functions

---

[12] Maria Nieto has suggested that the quality of supervision should also be taken into account in pricing banks' risk (Hardy & Nieto, 2008; see Eisenbeis & Kaufman, 2010, for a similar approach). However, within the European Union such an approach does not seem feasible, due to the resulting stigma on national supervisors. A viable alternative could be to give real teeth to the peer review of national supervisors now envisaged in the proposals before Council and Parliament for strengthened supervision in the EU. On a different line of argument, Achim Dübel has argued that it is not possible to have risk-based fees for deposit insurance without allowing for risk-based deductions from capital requirements – unless one is willing to envisage highly differentiated charges for deposit insurance. As we shall explain, this is precisely our approach.

[13] Masera (2009) stressed that there is a logical and operational continuum between crisis prevention and resolution and that it is hard to neatly separate the various phases of a banking crisis.

centralised with the parent company. This 'living wills' document may also comprise 'segregation' arrangements to preserve certain functions of systemic relevance even during resolution: for clearing and settlement of certain transactions, netting out of certain counterparties, suspension of covenants on certain operations (BCBS, 2009b, and Hüpkes, 2004).

In preparing their living wills, banks would be free to decide the structure and organisation of their business, notably regarding the decision to set up branches or subsidiaries in the foreign jurisdictions where they operate. However, separate resolution of subsidiaries, eschewing consolidation in the parent group, would only be allowed to the extent that they would be demonstrably fully independent of the parent company, would be unaffected by its liquidation and would not endanger its survival in case the subsidiary were wound up.

In sum, while we used to try and prevent bank failures, now the policy task should be to prepare for bank failures. Setting up such an apparatus requires that all national legislatures should adopt a set of common principles and administrative powers for early corrective action and resolution of a bank crisis, as has been recommended by the Basel Supervisors (BCBS, 2009b), but does not require full harmonisation of national laws.

Finally, the third pillar of an effectively reformed financial system is a set of procedural arrangements that will strongly discourage supervisory forbearance, and indeed make it unlikely. To this end it is necessary to establish a system of early mandated action by bank supervisors ensuring that, as capital falls below certain thresholds, the bank or banking group will be promptly and adequately recapitalized. Should the bank fail to do so and capital continue to fall, then supervisors would be empowered to step in and impose all necessary reorganisation, including disposing of assets, selling or closing lines of business, changing management, ceding the entire bank to a stronger entity.

Should this also not work, then liquidation would commence. A bridge bank would take over deposits and other "sound" banking activities, thus ensuring their continuity. All other assets and liabilities, together with the price received for the transfer of assets to the bridge bank, would remain in the "residual" bank, which would be stripped of its banking licence. An administrator for the liquidation of the residual bank would be appointed to determine its value and satisfy creditors according to the legal order of priorities, based on the law of the parent company and other jurisdictions involved.

Supervisory discretion to postpone corrective action would be strictly constrained, so that bankers, stakeholders and the public would know that mistakes would always meet early retribution. Mandated corrective action has another attractive feature: asset disposals and change of management would normally take place well before capital falls to zero, so that losses for the insurance fund and ultimately taxpayers would be greatly limited.

Within the European Union, the approach that has been described could be implemented through appropriate modification of the Directives on Deposit Guarantee Schemes (94/19/EC, 2009/14/EC), Reorganisation and Winding Up of credit institutions (2001/24/EC) and Capital Requirements (2006/48/EC), as will be described. Required changes would concern the following four aspects.

First, all cross-border banking groups would be required to sign up to a new deposit guarantee scheme managed by the European Banking Authority (henceforth EBA). The scheme would be fully funded ex-ante – albeit perhaps a share of the money, say 25%, could be withheld by banks and made available on call – by levying fees determined on an actuarial risk basis. Participating banks would undertake to provide all relevant information to the EBA and the Colleges of supervisors.

Second, all banking groups would be supervised, subjected to mandated corrective action, reorganised and, should the need arise, liquidated on a consolidated basis, under the law of the parent company; subsidiaries chartered in separate jurisdictions, but unable to survive a crisis of the parent company on their own, would also fall under the same authority.

Third, all national supervisors would have administrative powers to resolve banking groups according to the common principles already outlined by the Basel Supervisors.

Fourth, resolution of banking group in crisis would be managed by strengthened Colleges of supervisors, under the leadership of the parent company supervisor and a regime of full exchange of information amongst all interested national supervisors. The Colleges of supervisors would report to the EBA, under creation following the de Larosière Report recommendations, which would sanction all proposals by the Colleges with its own decisions. These decisions would include the initiation of early corrective action and all subsequent steps, and the mediation of disputes between national supervisors.

Introducing these changes would be no small feat; however, their necessity has been amply demonstrated by the momentous events of 2008. A few jurisdictions have already adopted some of the legislative principles illustrated above.

Placing the EBA at the centre of the system is especially important, since only in this way would all national supervisors and private interested parties be guaranteed of fair treatment, and thus be ready to accept the delegation of resolution powers to another jurisdiction. Mandated action would also give them the guarantee that supervisory forbearance would not be used to favour national interests in the parent company's jurisdictions to the detriment of other stakeholders.

The remainder of this report is organised as follows. Chapter 2 focuses on deposit insurance: after analysing its rationale and describing the main features of various schemes around the world and in the European Union, it proposes a new European system of deposit guarantee. Chapter 3 discusses bank resolution regimes and identifies the requisites that a new EU system should possess in order to re-establish a credible threat of bankruptcy in the financial system. Chapter 4 describes the weaknesses of the current supervisory arrangements at EU level and proposes the establishment of a new system founded on existing national supervisory structures by entrusting all key decisions to the EBA.

2. A EUROPEAN SYSTEM OF DEPOSIT GUARANTEE

Banks are 'special' financial intermediaries because they raise funds by accepting deposits redeemable on demand at par which perform, like currency, the functions of means of payment and store of value. The typically illiquid and longer-term nature of bank assets makes reimbursement of deposits difficult in case of sudden and simultaneous withdrawals by depositors; therefore banks are exposed to bank runs, which may be contagious and compromise trust in a main component of the money supply, endangering not only the banking system but the health of the entire economy.

To resolve this problem deposit insurance came to life in the United States in 1933, following a dramatic wave of panic which forced at one point all banks to shut down.[14] By limiting the danger that massive deposit withdrawals force banks to undertake a fire-sale of assets, deposit insurance is meant to eliminate a main source of systemic instability from financial systems.

The example of the United States was later followed by most other countries: by 2009, almost 100 countries had introduced a deposit guarantee scheme (Alessandri & Haldane, 2009; see Figure 2.1).

---

[14] See Calomiris (2000) for a detailed historical study on the origins of deposit insurance in the United States.

Figure 2.1 Adoption of deposit insurance and financial crises

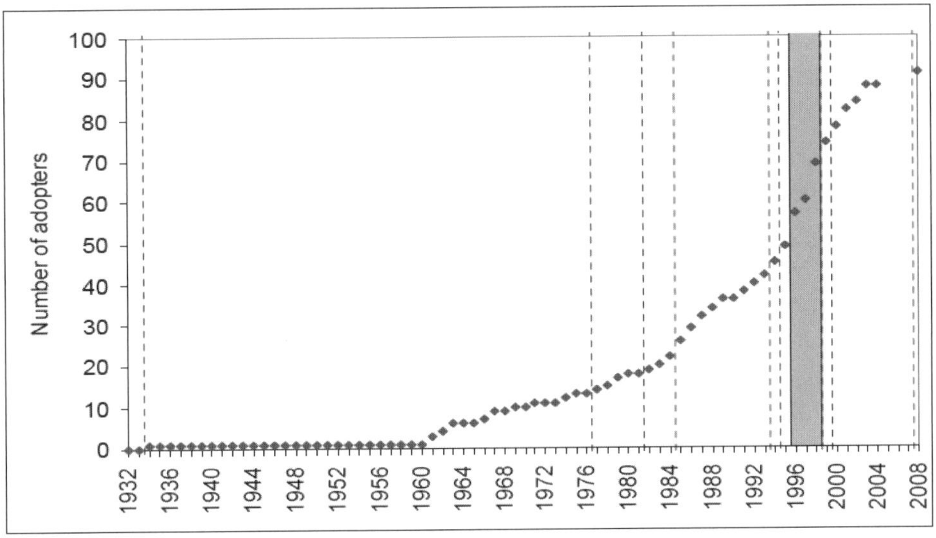

Trigger events: 1934 – Great Depression (US); 1977 – Banking crisis (Spain); 1982 – Banking crisis (Kuwait); 1985 – Banking crisis (Kenya); 1994 – Banking crises (Czech Republic, Uganda); 1995 – Banking crises (Brazil, Bulgaria); 1996 – Banking crises (Belarus, Lithuania); 1996-1998 – Asian crisis (Indonesia, Korea, Malaysia, Thailand); 1998 – Banking crisis (Ukraine).

Source: Alessandri & Haldane (2009).

Deposit insurance schemes have been effective in preventing bank runs – albeit not banking crises – the only exception in recent years being represented by Northern Rock.[15] However, it has its own drawbacks from the standpoint of financial stability since it weakens market discipline and creates moral hazard.[16] Depositors, reassured by the guarantee on the value of their deposits, have less incentive to monitor bank management and performance. Thus, management not only has greater room for undertaking risky activities, but greater inducement to risk depositors'

---

[15] For a detailed study on the Northern Rock crisis, see Eisenbeis & Kaufman (2009) and Llewellyn (2009).

[16] Demirgüç-Kunt & Detragiache (2002) found empirical evidence that deposit insurance has an adverse impact on bank stability, the more so the higher the coverage, where the scheme is pre-funded and where it is run by the government rather than by the private sector.

money in the expectation that any losses will be covered by the insurance fund and eventually taxpayers, while they will be able to keep for themselves a large chunk of the profits from risky bets. As a result, banks pay less dearly for money, while also benefiting at the same time from an implicit state subsidy on their speculative investments.

Thus, the design of an effective deposit insurance system involves a trade-off between conflicting objectives. On the one hand, insufficient protection may weaken depositors' confidence and raise the danger of a panic; on the other hand, a blanket protection may exacerbate moral hazard and compromise market discipline.[17]

In the United States, the crisis of the savings and loan (S&L) associations in the 1980s provided a startling example of how deposit insurance may remove the incentives for depositors to exercise proper monitoring of their banks and encourage management to free ride. S&L associations' shares had been granted deposit-like protection by the Federal Savings and Loan Insurance Corporation (FSLIC) in order to channel funds into mortgage lending. Cheap funding was used to acquire increasingly risky mortgages; and some S&L institutions also became heavily exposed to the high-yield 'junk' bond market (Chancellor, 1999). The sharp increase in interest rates of the early 1980s pushed large parts of the system over the brink. Rather than applying its regulatory powers to bring losses out in the open, the S&L regulator, the Federal Home Loan Bank Board (FHLBB), relaxed capital requirements to gain time. Supervisory forbearance was encouraged by the insufficient pool of resources available to the FHLBB to prop up troubled institutions. The combined cost of reckless bankers' behaviour and regulatory forbearance finally amounted to an astounding $150 billion and the FSLIC became insolvent and was shut down.[18]

While policy blunders were probably responsible for precipitating the crisis, the run on Northern Rock in September 2007 has highlighted the risk of an ill-designed deposit insurance scheme. Northern Rock had aggressively expanded its balance sheet and built a large portfolio of

---

[17] On the conflict between these opposing public policy goals and on an incentive compatible design of deposit insurance, see Beck (2004).

[18] On the S&L crisis, see Benston & Kaufman (1997) and Kane (1989, 1993).

mortgages[19] largely funded on the wholesale money market. The increase in interest rates and the seizing up of the securitisation market hampered its ability to roll over its short-term debt. The news that the Bank of England was extending emergency liquidity assistance to Northern Rock triggered the first bank run in the UK since 1866 (Overend & Gurney; see Kindleberger & Aliber, 2005; and Bruner & Carr, 2007).

However, a main reason for depositors' fears seems to have been the limited protection provided by the UK deposit insurance scheme, characterised not only by a low coverage (deposits only up to £35,000), but also by a co-insurance mechanism whereby a percentage of losses (10%) would be borne by insured deposits above the minimum amount of £2,000 (Schich, 2008). There were also doubts about the adequacy of the insurance fund to cover potential losses on insured deposits, and fears that in all events payments would be subject to long and unpredictable delays, causing both credit and liquidity losses. In particular, co-insurance apparently failed in making depositors more aware of their risks, indicating perhaps that retail depositors cannot be relied upon as a source of market discipline (Eisenbeis & Kaufman, 2009).

Together with the importance of adequate funding, the crisis of Icelandic banks in October 2008 shed light on another critical feature of deposit insurance, i.e. cross-border arrangements. The three major Icelandic banks, Glitnir, Landsbanki and Kaupthing, had subsidiaries and branches in several European countries (including the UK, the Netherlands and Germany) where deposits had grown out of proportion thanks to over-generous returns. Depositors were in principle protected by the Icelandic insurance which, however, had negligible resources relative to ballooning deposits. When depositors rushed for the exit, the banks could not meet their obligations; the UK authorities froze the assets of UK branches,[20] while their parent companies were nationalised by the Icelandic government. Their losses represent such a high share of Iceland's GDP that repayment is unlikely.

---

[19] Total assets more than doubled from £42 billion in 2004 to £109 billion in 2007 and the bank's share in the UK mortgage lending market increased from 6% in 1999 to 19% in 2007 (Bank of England, 2007).

[20] Interestingly, the legal basis for the freezing was the 2001 Anti-Terrorism, Crime and Security Act, passed after September 11, 2001. See Buiter & Sibert (2008) for a detailed study on the Icelandic banking crisis.

In sum, deposit insurance is an effective system to eliminate bank runs from the financial landscape, but its rules and mechanisms must be carefully designed so as to tread a safe course between the opposite dangers of inadequate protection lacking credibility and excessive protection subsidising reckless risk-taking. Cross-border banking complicates the matter further by raising doubts about the effectiveness of protection and eventual responsibility for the losses.

2.1 Confidence, financial stability and deposit insurance

Deposit insurance schemes were introduced to protect banks and the integrity of certain functions, such as the payment system, at a time when the role of banks was substantially confined to deposit-taking and commercial lending. Since depository banks operate on the basis of a fractional reserve system, they perform a key function in the multiplication of monetary base and the transmission of monetary policy impulses.

In the last four decades, the forces of deregulation, conglomeration and globalisation have deeply transformed the role of banks in the financial system, eroding the barriers between banking, insurance and the securities business. Legal geographical and functional restrictions on banks have been removed, notably in the US with the 1999 Gramm-Leach-Bliley Act and in the European Union with the Second Banking Directive (89/646/EEC).

As a consequence, the optimal design of deposit insurance has changed. In the traditional specialised environment, the protection of depositors and public trust in fiduciary money naturally coincided with the stability of banks: drawing the line within banks' balance sheets between what deserved protection and what did not was not an issue. With banks competing for non-bank business, the twin question arises: on one hand, should deposit insurance de facto protect the banks themselves or should it instead concentrate on the protection of depositors alone? On the other hand, should insurance also be extended to non-bank intermediaries issuing monetary liabilities (e.g. money market mutual funds and commercial paper)?[21] The critical aspect in deciding this issue is that, as has

---

[21] In the United States in September and October 2008, the Federal Reserve introduced facilities of money market mutual funds and the commercial paper market (see Di Noia & Micossi, 2009).

been discussed, any explicit or implicit guarantee may encourage reckless risk-taking. On the other hand, financial supervisors are even less keen on letting financial institutions fail in the wake of the disastrous consequences of Lehman Brothers' collapse.

The large exposure of non-depository financial institutions to banks gave governments and central bankers a strong reason to bail out troubled non-bank financial institutions in order to preserve the banks. This was the case for AIG, which had sold massive amounts of credit default swaps to European banks, which had bought them for regulatory capital relief and would have been hardly hit by the collapse of AIG.[22] Similarly, investment banks were over-exposed in the wholesale money market, where the main source of funds is constituted by very short-term bank credit lines (e.g. repos). De facto, all non-bank financial intermediation was 'banking' on the guarantee that banks would not be allowed to fail.

This spurious extension of deposit guarantee to non-bank activities was even more blatant within bank holding companies, which were channelling depositors' money to support their forays into high-yield market activities. Thus, complexity and interconnectedness were to a large extent the result of operations designed to spread the benefits of banking charters to most financial intermediation.

A proposed solution to overcome the moral hazard problem is to revert to narrow banking, in the most extreme versions by imposing the condition that all money raised as deposits could only be invested in safe assets (Kay, 2009). In practice this would be equivalent to a 100% reserve requirement on all deposits, entailing of course that the money multiplier mechanism would be removed from the financial system and credit would be made available only from existing savings – thus entailing a sharp contraction in lending. Also, a strictly narrow banking system would eliminate monetary policy since "public debt held by banks would set the

---

[22] See Di Noia & Micossi (2009) and Gros & Micossi (2008). As stated in the AIG 2007 annual report: "Approximately $379 billion (consisting of the corporate loans and prime residential mortgages) of the $527 billion in notional exposure of AIGFP's super senior credit default swap portfolio as of December 31, 2007 represents derivatives written for financial institutions, principally in Europe, for the purpose of providing them with regulatory capital relief rather than risk mitigation."

money supply".[23] Moreover, efficiency gains from diversification and economies of scale and scope might be lost.[24]

It should be noted, at all events, that this approach does not require legal or structural separation of narrow banking from financial activities, but only that within each bank or banking group deposit-taking and associated portfolio investments are segregated functionally. All room for using deposit money for speculative capital market activities would be effectively removed from the system (for an overview of the pros and cons of narrow banking, see Box 2.1).[25]

Box 2.1 Narrow banking

There is no unique and unanimously accepted definition of narrow banking. Conceptually, narrow banking entails restricting the activities that banks are allowed to perform so as to separate deposit-taking and, in some versions, commercial lending from all other activities, with a view to eliminating or strictly limiting any maturity mismatch and liquidity risk when investing depositors' money. In the strictest versions where deposit proceeds are invested in perfectly safe and liquid assets, deposit insurance becomes superfluous – except in the case of outright fraud.

➤ There are two broad categories of narrow banking restrictions, i.e. a) on assets maturity: only short-term safe assets or short-term as well as long-term safe assets; and b) on lending activity (prohibition or limitations).

➤ Three proposed models of narrow banking:

   a) Financial institutions draw a legal distinction between monetary service companies and financial service companies. Monetary service companies may accept deposits, provide payment services and are

---

[23] Martin Wolf, "Why narrow banking alone is not the finance solution", *Financial Times*, 29 September 2008.

[24] However, there is no clear evidence of these potential benefits related to financial conglomeration; see Laeven & Levine (2006) and Schinasi (2009).

[25] See Kay (2009) and King (2009). Di Noia (1994) provides an interesting variation of the narrow banking model, the 'narrow-narrow banking' model, according to which banks should only invest in safe assets the 100% of the positive difference between the total amount of deposit insured and the total compulsory reserves; the banking activity would thus be less restricted than in the classic narrow banking model.

permitted to invest only in short-term, highly marketable and highly rated instruments, such as short-term Treasury securities (and perhaps top-rated commercial paper). Financial service companies can perform all other financial activities (Pierce, 1991).

b) Financial holding company can operate banking subsidiaries and separately incorporated lending subsidiaries; banking subsidiaries can invest in short-term and long-term safe and highly liquid securities (Litan, 1987).

c) Financial holding company with bank subsidiaries and lending subsidiaries: bank subsidiaries are allowed to invest in a wide range of safe assets and to engage in some form of commercial lending, e.g. loans to small firms. In this model the narrow bank is involved in credit creation (Bryan, 1991).

➢ All these versions of narrow banking are 'narrower' than the Glass-Steagall-style separation of commercial banking and investment banking. The narrow bank model separates lending and deposit-taking functions, even though this is softened when the narrow bank is part of a group that also performs lending activity through other subsidiaries.

➢ **Pros of narrow banking**: elimination or minimisation of liquidity and maturity risks; minimal capital needs; no need for further regulation or safety net; deposit insurance only for risk of fraud; no moral hazard for bankers and fully restored incentive for investors in investment banks and in other financial institutions to monitor management behaviour.

➢ **Cons of narrow banking**: no benefits from maturity and liquidity transformation; no efficiency gains and synergy effects from joint production of lending and deposit-taking; no money multiplier and limits to credit growth; in countries with sound public finances and low government debt, need to issue public debt in support of monetary and payment services; unsophisticated depositors only protected when they invest their savings in deposits; unknown implementing costs for lack of empirical evidence.

Some policy-makers and commentators consider that the only feasible solution to tackle moral hazard and the 'too-big-to-fail' problem is to cut down by decree all large financial organisations to a size that no longer threatens systemic stability, or legally separate commercial and investment banking, or make illegal proprietary trading by deposit banks. The US authorities have announced the introduction of a size limit that would cover all firms that control one or more insured depository institutions, as well as other major financial firms that are so large and interconnected as to fall within the new regime of consolidated, comprehensive supervision (White House, 2010; Wolin, 2010).

Paul Volcker (Volcker, 2010) has advocated that all FDIC depository institutions, as well as any firm that controls an FDIC-insured depository institution, should be prevented from engaging in proprietary trading, and from owning or sponsoring private equity funds or hedge funds (now commonly referred to as the 'Volker rule'). The rationale of this proposal is to prevent non-bank financial institutions from free-riding on the safety net provided by central banks and regulators to commercial banks in view of the essential functions they perform. The US government has now subscribed to the Volcker rule (White House, 2010; Wolin, 2010).

An alternative approach – in our view much preferable to narrow banking and the Volcker rule – would be to let banks continue to perform their broad range of functions but restrict insurance exclusively to depositors, which is needed to preserve confidence in money. In principle, this is precisely how US deposit insurance was meant to work.

Well designed deposit insurance capable of making depositors feel safe but leaving all other bank creditors out in the cold would in practice achieve the same result as narrow banking – while avoiding its pitfalls. Of course, this approach would only be effective to the extent that explicit or implicit guarantee on any bank liability other than deposits were credibly ruled out – including short-term credit lines from other banks, bonds and shares. This principle should be embedded into legislation so that neither regulators nor national governments would be able to break or circumvent the rule.

Under this approach banks would be free to undertake capital market activities as they judged fit, while shareholders and lenders of the bank would have a much stronger incentive to monitor management and the bank's activities, since they would be fully exposed to the losses from excessive risk-taking, and they would know it. The preference granted to depositors would eliminate all uncertainty on the perimeter of the safety net.

This was indeed the philosophy underlying the FDIC system (see Box 2.2). It has failed in practice because some banks covered by the system were allowed to grow so large and undertake such massive risks that the available funds became irrelevant, relative to the size of emerging losses. The only alternative then was to extend a blanket guarantee to the financial institutions themselves.

Box 2.2 The US Federal Deposit Insurance system

Deposit insurance was introduced in the United States by the Glass-Steagall Banking Act of 1933, which established the Federal Deposit Insurance Corporation (FDIC). The FDIC received an initial capital endowment of $289 million from the US Treasury and the Federal Reserve. Until 1990 the FDIC charged flat insurance fees of approximately 8.3 cents per $100 of insured deposits. In 1980 the deposit insurance fund was given a target range of 1.1% to 1.4% of total insured deposits, but the massive savings and loans losses depleted the fund. In 1989 the Financial Institutions Reform, Recovery, and Enforcement Act (FIRREA) mandated that premia be raised to bring the fund up to 1.25% of insured deposits.

In 1991 the Federal Deposit Insurance Corporation Improvement Act (FDICIA) introduced a system of risk-based fees, to be calculated on the basis of capitalisation and the supervisory rating: three capitalisation categories (well capitalised, adequately capitalised and undercapitalised) and three supervisory rating groups (rating of 1 or 2, rating of 3, rating of 4 or 5) were established. For large institutions in the lowest risk category other factors are also considered for risk-assessment, including the rating of long-term debt, market data, financial performance indicators, the ability of an institution to withstand financial stress and loss severity indicators (see FDIC, 2009). From 1990 to 2006, over 90% of banks were classified in the lowest risk category (well capitalised and with a rating of 1 or 2). Moreover, the FDICIA and the Deposit Insurance Act of 1996 decided that the banks in the lowest risk category should not pay deposit insurance fees if the fund reserves were above 1.25% of insured deposits, which was the case throughout the period 1996-2006. In this decade, therefore, most banks did not pay deposit insurance.

The FDICIA also introduced the system of prompt corrective action, which mandated the FDIC to intervene to impose recapitalisation on ailing banks well before full depletion of capital, with powers to close the institutions if they fail to do so. These interventions must respect the condition of least cost for the deposit insurance fund, unless a 'systemic risk exception' is invoked, which requires approval by at least two-thirds of the FDIC Board, two-thirds of the Federal Reserve Board, and the US Treasury Secretary after consultation with the US President.

The Federal Deposit Insurance Reform Act of 2005 substituted the 'hard' target of 1.25% of insured deposits with a 1.15% to 1.50% range, and decided that when the fund exceeds 1.35% of insured deposits, 50% of the surplus is restituted to the member; when it exceeds 1.50%, the totality of excess funds are restituted. On the other hand, when fund reserves fall below 1.15%, the FDIC must raise premia to a level sufficient to restore them to this minimum level.

During the financial crisis of 2007-09, the deposit insurance reserves progressively fell, going down to 1.01% of insured deposits on 30 June 2008, to 0.36% in the last quarter of 2008, and to 0.22% on 30 June 2009; the deposit insurance fund reserve ratio even became negative, at -0.16% on 30 September 2009.

On 22 May 2009, the FDIC board approved a final rule that imposed a 5 basis points special assessment as of 30 June 2009 and on 29 September 2009 the FDIC adopted an Amended Restoration Plan to replenish the fund and raise the reserve ratio up to 1.15% within eight years. To this end, insured institutions were required to prepay their estimated quarterly risk-based assessments for the fourth quarter of 2009, and for all of 2010, 2011, and 2012. At the same time, the FDIC raised annual risk-based assessment rates by 3 basis points beginning in 2011.

In 2009 the FDIC also obtained an increase in the credit line from the US Treasury from $30 billion to $100 billion, which can be raised to $500 billion with the approval of the Federal Reserve and the US President.

FDIC deposit insurance fund reserve ratio (2006-2009; % of insured deposits)

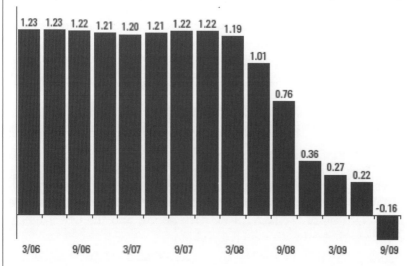

Source: FDIC (2009).

Overall, historical experience of the FDIC deposit insurance demonstrates on the one hand that flat deposit insurance fees are ineffective to ensure the protection of the fund and its viability when a crisis occurs, and on the other hand that a system of risk-based fees does not automatically solve the problems. In fact, it has to be carefully drafted to make the fund as resilient as possible to crises and actually able to perform its function of deposit protection. To this purpose, a key objective is to avoid the pro-cyclicality of the balance of the fund, whereby the fund is in good shape in good times, but is rapidly exhausted in bad times: the assessment of the risk profile of banks and the proper pricing of deposit insurance are the key tools.

Sources: Acharya, Santos and Yorulmazer (2009), FDIC (2009) and Pennacchi (2009).

2.2 Key ingredients of deposit insurance

In order to maintain market discipline and eschew moral hazard, the threat whereby the banks will not be rescued, only the depositors, needs additional foundation in the design of the deposit insurance system.

Market discipline may be enhanced and moral hazard contained by introducing certain limitations on depositors' coverage (BCBS & IADI, 2009). First, as has been indicated, protection should be granted only to retail depositors, while wholesale and interbank deposits would be at lenders' risk. Second, retail depositors should not enjoy full protection – albeit not so low as to compromise confidence – in order to keep them awake to the risk features of their banks. The amount set in the revised EU Deposit Guarantee Directive, €50,000 rising to €100,000, seems adequate.[26] As to co-insurance, it should not play a major role, since any positive effect on depositors' willingness to monitor the bank's performance and management may be offset by adverse effects on their confidence, as highlighted by the run on Northern Rock.

---

[26] Directive 2009/14/EC of 11 March 2009. Article 1, 3(a) envisages an increase of the coverage from €50,000 to €100,000 by 31 December 2010, unless the Commission determines that "such an increase and such harmonisation are inappropriate and not financially viable for all Member States in order to ensure consumer protection and financial stability in the Community and avoid cross-border distortions between Member States".

A critical feature is the size and financing of the insurance fund. The 2007-09 financial crisis showed that deposit insurance schemes financed ex-post, that is only after the need materialises, lack credibility because the deposit insurance fund is likely to be undercapitalised. Only ex-ante financing, based on probabilistic assessment of the risk of failure for each insured bank, appears capable of ensuring at the same time that the fund has sufficient resources and that each insured bank pays a fee commensurate with its actual risk position, hence the potential cost of its failure, thus mitigating moral hazard (BCBS & IADI, 2009) and strengthening depositors' incentive to monitor the bank. Ex-ante financing is also less pro-cyclical than a call-when-needed system, which imposes higher costs when banks' profitability is falling.[27]

The fund should be required to meet its funding targets within a specified time period; premia should be collected and the fund should continue to grow even after the funding target is reached. The US system of returning premia once the funding target has been reached appears logically flawed – one doesn't return insurance premia because the adverse event did not materialise – and is strongly pro-cyclical, with funds likely to be in excess in fair weather and insufficient in crisis (see Box 2.2).

Risk assessment must reflect institution-specific factors – including not only size and asset quality, but a wide range of factors such as capitalisation, liquidity and maturity transformation, the quality of management and risk control, interconnectedness, complexity, functions of systemic relevance such as being a major supplier of CDS or offering clearing services for significant market segments. Fees should also take account of the bank's exposure to systemic risks (based on stress tests) as well its likely impact on systemic risk in case of adverse macroeconomic

---

[27] A key point to be emphasised in this connection is that the deposit insurance fund should be designed to deal with bank crises in 'fair weather'; in the event of a systemic collapse no amount would suffice, short of full government guarantee (although the different components of the safety net should be capable of interacting through close coordination and information-sharing in such a crisis; see BCBS & IADI, 2009). Therefore, the size of the fund is much lower than the overall amount of insured deposits in a given country (e.g. between 1.15% and 1.50% in the United States; see Gros, 2009).

shocks.[28] Higher fees, in this context, could be required from banks operating in 'overbanked countries', e.g. showing high ratios of bank liabilities over GDP or the total tax base as indicators of local ability to take emerging losses in a crisis.

It has been suggested in this context that the CDS spread already provides a synthetic measure of the default risk and therefore could be used directly to determine the insurance fee as a proportion of insured deposits. However, back-of-the-envelope calculations suggest that the resulting charge could be too onerous and wipe out all banking profits.[29] Therefore, while the CDS may well be one important element in the calculation, it appears preferable to set fees on the basis of several factors, also including sustainability of the banking system. It must be well understood, however, that a considerable reduction in bank profits is a desirable feature of the insurance scheme, since inordinate profits from speculation played a paramount role in diverting resources away from the productive economy and into unproductive speculative activities.

It should be stressed, in this context, that the objective of risk-based fees is not to penalise depository banks and banking groups for the deposit-taking activity itself. Rather, it is to make banks pay the appropriate price for the banking charter and the related benefits (deposit insurance, access to discount window, etc.), based on the overall risk profile of the bank.[30]

---

[28] Maino et al. (2009) propose a new approach to regulation and resolution of Systemically Important Financial Institutions (SIFIs) and argue that systemic risk should be covered by an ad hoc "insurance premium" for SIFIs, to be paid as fees to a specific Resolution Fund.

[29] John Kay, "Why 'too big to fail' insurance will not fix finance", *Financial Times*, 3 February 2010.

[30] The US Financial Crisis Responsibility Fee, recently announced in January 2010 by the US President to recover the public resources injected to rescue and stabilise the financial sector, is based on a different logic. It applies to banks and other categories of financial institutions with more than $50 billion in consolidated assets and will be levied for at least 10 years. The fee is calculated as a proportion (about 0.15%) of banks liabilities. Tier 1 capital and insured deposits are deducted from the computation, the latter being regarded as a stable source of funding and already paid for through deposit insurance fees. Thus, this fee would penalise those banks with a thinner deposit base and less capital. The underlying

To the extent that fees asked from large banks were adequate to deal with their failure, one main aspect of the too-big-to-fail syndrome, as identified by Acharya (2009) and Kay (2009), would be, if not eliminated, at least substantially reduced.[31] If appropriately designed, these fees would entail a strong disincentive against growing too large.

Risk-based deposit insurance seems to offer a superior tool for charging banks the correct price for their banking charter, regulatory protection and potential losses, also by taking into account immaterial factors that risk-based capital charges cannot reflect, but supervisors can fully consider thanks to their access to the whole of bank information.[32] It would overcome the problem of distinguishing between systemic and non-systemic banks since fees would gradually and continuously increase with risk (FSA, 2009b); there would be no need to set up a separate layer of regulation and charges for 'systemic' banks.

Banks would still be required to hold capital as general reserve against unexpected losses and restraint against excessive risk-taking by management. However, capital requirements should be set as a straight minimum ratio to total assets or liabilities – net of net worth – with no allowance for risk factors.

A key complement of deposit insurance is mandated corrective action by supervisors as bank capital falls below certain thresholds. Moral hazard and the potential costs for the fund are exacerbated if there is no mandated corrective action, because banks exploit the deposit insurance subsidy to engage in excessive risk-taking and will try to delay recognition of losses and to gamble for resurrection. Authorities could complacently favour such behaviour and even relax regulation in the hope of facilitating a recovery.

---

assumption is that a lower core capital buffer and higher reliance on non-deposit funding imply higher overall risk.

[31] For a discussion of systemic risk premiums versus the breaking-up of large financial institutions, see Acharya, Cooley, Richardson & Walter (2009).

[32] The US CAMELS ratings provide an interesting model usable for this purpose, whereby a bank risk profile is assessed on Capital, Assets, Management, Earnings, Liquidity and Sensitivity to risk. A question to be decided in this context is whether or not risk-assessments and deposit guarantee fees should be made public. Disclosure might enhance market discipline but also damage confidence in the bank. The US CAMELS are non-public information and property of the supervisory authorities.

Besides, the subsidised institutions are presumably those that are the least worth saving, so that forbearance produces the undesirable outcome of wasting taxpayers' money in the most inefficient manner.[33]

Ultimately, gambling for resurrection and forbearance would amplify the losses for the deposit insurance fund and could deplete its financial resources and hinder its ability to protect depositors. Therefore, mandated corrective action is essential in order to ensure the credibility of deposit insurance.[34]

2.3   An overview of deposit guarantee schemes

Deposit guarantee schemes came under enormous pressure worldwide in the wake of the financial crisis, which highlighted their weaknesses. In September 2008, Ireland decided – without consulting the European Commission, the European Central bank or any of the EU member states – to increase the statutory limit for the deposit guarantee scheme for banks and building societies from €20,000 to €100,000 per depositor per institution, with a 100% coverage for each individual deposit. Initially, it tried to cover only depositors at Irish banks but renounced this obvious discrimination almost immediately and offered the guarantee to certain subsidiaries of foreign institutions operating within its jurisdiction. Massive cross-border flights of deposits from neighbouring countries prompted an increase in coverage throughout Europe, in some cases with a formally higher coverage threshold, in others (e.g. Germany) with a political commitment to unlimited deposits protection (Figure 2.2). State guarantees were soon extended also to bank liabilities other than deposits (including bonds, interbank deposits, commercial paper).

More or less the same happened in the United States, where the FDIC deposit insurance was temporarily raised from $100,000 to $250,000 and

---

[33] For an analysis of the S&Ls crisis that reaches these conclusions, see Calomiris, Klingebiel & Laeven (2005).

[34] Benston & Kaufman (1988) first advocated the need for a system of early intervention in the United States, which was then introduced in 1991 by the Federal Deposit Insurance Corporation Improvement Act. See Chapter 4 of this report for an in-depth analysis of mandated corrective action with specific focus on the European Union.

guarantees were introduced on certain other bank liabilities. Australia and New Zealand also decided to introduce deposit insurance (Schich, 2009).

In November 2009 the International Association of Deposit Insurers and the International Monetary Fund presented a report to the Financial Stability Board (FSB) on the unwinding of deposit insurance arrangements adopted in response to the global financial crisis (IADI & IMF, 2009).

Figure 2.2 Coverage level of deposit guarantee schemes in selected countries (US $)

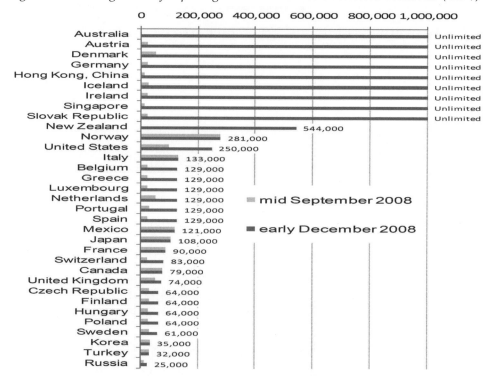

Source: Schich (2009).

Their report shows that 46 jurisdictions have adopted some form of enhancement of depositors' protection: 18 countries introduced full deposit guarantees, while 28 raised coverage either permanently or temporarily (see Table 2.1).

Table 2.1 Actions adopted to strengthen deposit guarantee schemes

Full depositor guarantees	Deposit guarantee coverage increase	
	Permanent	**Temporary**
Austria	Albania	Australia
Denmark	Belgium	Brazil
Germany[1]	Bulgaria	Netherlands
Greece[1]	Croatia	New Zealand[8]
Hong Kong, SAR	Cyprus	Switzerland
Hungary[1]	Czech Republic	Ukraine
Iceland[1]	Estonia	United States[4]
Ireland[7]	Finland	
Jordan	Indonesia	
Kuwait[3]	Latvia	
Malaysia	Lithuania	
Mongolia[3]	Luxembourg	
Portugal[1]	Kazakhstan[2]	
Singapore	Malta	
Slovakia[6]	Philippines	
Slovenia[3]	Poland	
Thailand	Romania	
UAE[5]	Russia	
	Spain	
	Sweden	
	United Kingdom	

[1] Political commitments by government.

[2] Increased from 700,000 to 5 million tenge but will revert to 1 million on 1/1/2012.

[3] Unlimited for banks operating in their jurisdiction.

[4] Unlimited for non-interest-bearing transaction accounts.

[5] Unlimited for local and foreign banks with significant presence in their jurisdiction.

[6] Unlimited for all physical persons and some categories of legal persons.

[7] Unlimited for seven specific banks representing 80% of the banking system.

[8] Full coverage up to NZ$1 million per deposit (retail deposits and non-bank deposit takers).

Source: IADI & IMF (2009).

In the European Union, the Deposit Guarantee Schemes Directive adopted in 1994 (94/19/EC) had established a minimum level of coverage per depositor equal to €20,000, leaving actual coverage to the discretion of member states, but at all events excluding interbank deposits. It included an option for member states to have co-insurance, with a minimum floor of 90%. Overall, the Directive did not manage to bring about sufficient harmonisation regarding coverage, funding, co-insurance, and who should operate the scheme (private agency versus public authority); as a result, national systems have remained highly heterogeneous. A largely common element is that at least in principle deposit insurance is financed by banks; however, the principle is negated by the weakness of funding arrangements that make the system credible only for small-size interventions.

Table 2.2 shows the main features of deposit guarantee schemes in selected countries as of 2007 (that is, pre-crisis): as may be seen, a majority of countries had premiums collected ex-ante (two main exceptions being Italy and the United Kingdom); co-insurance was present in less than half of the countries; in most cases deposit insurance fees were flat and not risk-based.

The European Commission had taken into consideration a review of the Deposit Guarantee Directive in the years preceding the 2007-09 crisis, but no substantial amendments had been proposed before the crisis struck in 2008. On 7 October 2008, the Ecofin Council agreed to raise the minimum level of deposit coverage to a minimum of €50,000 and up to €100,000. On October 15 the European Commission presented a plan to review Directive 94/19/EC whose main proposals were: i) to increase minimum coverage level to €50,000, and to €100,000 after one year;[35] ii) to abandon co-insurance and iii) to minimise the payout period (from the current three months, extendible to nine). These changes were introduced by Directive 2009/14/EC of 11 March 2009.

The responsibility for deposit guarantee amongst EU member states follows the home country principle: deposits at foreign branches of credit institutions headquartered in the member states are covered by the deposit guarantee scheme of the home country, while deposits at foreign subsidiaries are covered by the deposit guarantee scheme of the host country.

---

[35] About 65% of eligible deposits were covered under the previous regime; the new levels cover an estimated 80% (with coverage of €50,000) and 90% (with coverage of €100,000) of deposits.

Table 2.2 Main features of deposit guarantee schemes in selected countries (2007)

	Ex-ante collection of premia	Co-insurance	Risk-based deposit insurance fees
Austria	No	No	No
Belgium	Yes	No	Yes
Bulgaria	Yes	No	No
Cyprus	Yes	No	No
Czech Republic	Yes	Yes	No
Denmark	Yes	No	No
Estonia	Yes	Yes	No
Finland	Yes	No	Yes
France	Yes	No	Yes
Germany	ex ante and ex post	Yes	No
Greece	Yes	No	No
Hungary	Yes	Yes	Yes
Iceland	Yes	Yes	No
Ireland	Yes	Yes	No
Italy	No	No	Yes
Latvia	Yes	No	No
Lithuania	Yes	Yes	No
Luxembourg	No	No	No
Malta	ex ante and ex post	Yes	No
Netherlands	No	No	No
Norway	ex ante and ex post	No	Yes
Poland	ex ante and ex post	Yes	No
Portugal	Yes	Yes	Yes
Romania	Yes	No	Yes
Slovak Republic	Yes	Yes	No
Slovenia	No	No	No
Spain	Yes	No	No
Sweden	Yes	No	No
Switzerland	No	No	No
United Kingdom	No	Yes	No
United States	Yes	No	Yes

Source: Barth et al. (2008).

This allocation of tasks mirrors the division of responsibilities between home and host country for prudential supervision,[36] whereas the consolidated supervision of banking groups is assigned to the home country, while the host country only supervises locally chartered subsidiaries on a 'solo' basis and has very limited oversight on branches (on liquidity). Moreover, if the level or scope of the coverage of the host country deposit guarantee scheme is higher than that provided by the home country, a foreign branch may voluntarily join the host country scheme for supplementary guarantee (topping-up). On the other hand, when the coverage offered by the home country is higher, an issue of competitive disadvantage for institutions chartered in the host country may arise.

This setting leaves host countries exposed to the banking risks that may arise from foreign branches and subsidiaries due to a crisis of the parent bank, without endowing them with adequate lines of defence. With regard to subsidiaries, their soundness critically depends on the home country authority responsible for consolidated supervision and on confidence in the soundness of the parent bank: thus, the host country deposit guarantee fund would have to bear the costs of a bank run on a foreign subsidiary, but the host country would face constraints in the prevention phase since its supervisory powers are confined to oversight on a solo basis.[37] Risks may be especially intense for branches with systemic relevance in the host country that however represent only a small operation for the parent bank and home supervisors: this asymmetry between defence instruments and exposure to risk and the misalignment of incentives give rise to potential conflicts between the home and host country (Eisenbeis & Kaufman, 2006; Herring, 2007).

---

[36] For a detailed analysis of the EU allocation of supervision and deposit guarantee tasks to home and host country see Mayes et al. (2007).

[37] A possible solution would be to limit cross-border banking through branches and to increase national powers to require 'subsidiarisation', as suggested by the Turner Review (FSA, 2009a): this solution, however, could compromise the EU internal market and would also restrict banks' freedom in the choice of their corporate structure.

2.4   The way forward: a European Deposit Guarantee System

The existing arrangements for deposit guarantee schemes in the European Union turned out to be insufficient and ineffective; and there was a misalignment between the national nature of deposit guarantee schemes and the cross-border dimension of large European banks. The different coverage of depositors, depending on the nationality of the bank, creates an uneven playing field and gives rise to potential competitive inequality, and the topping-up for branches does not appear a sufficient tool to address the problem. Besides, as observed by the de Larosière Group (2009), no national deposit guarantee scheme would currently be able to make reimbursements to depositors of any large EU cross-border financial institution without the involvement of public funds.

The de Larosière report underlined that the lack of sophisticated and risk-sensitive funding arrangements "involves a significant risk that governments will have to carry the financial burden ... for the banks or worse, that the deposit guarantee scheme fails on their commitments (both of which were illustrated by the Icelandic case)". Moreover, they maintained that reliance on ex-post funding without risk-sensitive premiums entails moral hazard and is likely to distort the efficient allocation of deposits.

The rational response is the creation of a European deposit guarantee scheme capable of protecting depositors of large pan-European banks without creating fresh room for arbitrage or distortions owing to the different features of national schemes. A new system should include all the elements of well-designed deposit guarantee, as have been described: protection limited to retail deposits, ex-ante risk-based financing of the deposit guarantee fund and mandated corrective action. All large EU cross-border banking groups[38] should join the new EU scheme, while other banks could remain with national protection schemes, if they so wished. The heart of the EU system would be a new European Deposit Guarantee Agency (EDGA), entrusted with the management of a European Deposit Guarantee Fund (EDGF). The EDGA and the EDGF should be established within the

---

[38] Pan-European banking groups might be identified on the basis of a wide range of factors, including assets, revenues, net income, deposits, number of branches and subsidiaries.

European Banking Authority; the EU Deposit Guarantee Directive[39] and the proposed EBA Regulation should thus be amended to incorporate the new body and its fund. A network approach – entailing the creation of a European System of Deposit Guarantee Schemes, modelled on the European System of Central Banks and having the EDGA at its centre – would also be an option.

The EDGF should be pre-funded, with risk-based fees collected by the EDGA. Fees should be calculated in a way that ensures the capacity and credibility of the fund in protecting depositors of large European banks in case of failure. However, the fund should be able to guarantee depositor protection in 'fair weather', not in a systemic crisis, which instead would have to be managed in a coordinated manner by all the components of the safety net. The calculation of the fees is the key: risk assessments should take into account both the individual risk profile of banks and their systemic relevance, as has been described.

All retail deposits of pan-European banking groups would have to be guaranteed under the EU scheme, regardless of their geographical location (i.e. including deposits outside the EU). Clearly, pan-European banking groups would not have to pay deposit guarantee fees twice, but only at the EU level. To avoid distortions and an uneven playing field between pan-EU and domestic-oriented banking groups, national deposit guarantee schemes should be organised on the basis of the same rules of the European scheme.

To ensure the effectiveness and credibility of deposit guarantee, a target ratio of the deposit guarantee fund balance in proportion of total insured deposits should be established. The target ratio might be chosen on the basis of historical data on banking crises and the estimated actuarial risk of bank failures. Rather than as a 'hard' limit, it might be conceived as a 'safety range' with fees for participating banks falling when the upper range limit is exceeded and rising when the lower range is trespassed. In any event, restitution of funds to the participating banks should be

---

[39] Directive 2009/14/EC of 11 March 2009 (new Article 12 of Directive 94/19/EC) required the Commission to present a report and, if necessary, to put forward proposals to amend the Deposit Guarantee Directive in regard of a range of issues which include possible models for introducing risk-based contributions. The Joint Research Centre (European Commission) published in June 2009 a report on possible models for deposit guarantee risk-based contributions (JRC, 2009).

excluded since this would weaken the fund's ability to meet a rare crisis of a very large bank.

Another key feature of the proposed EU deposit guarantee system is that it should not have power to recapitalise or bail out failing institutions.[40] Open bank assistance instruments, like those that had been assigned in the United States to the FDIC, are not necessary: the assignment to EDGA of any of these instruments would be inconsistent with the philosophy of the proposed scheme, centred on protecting depositors and not financial institutions.[41] As a consequence, the revised Deposit Guarantee Directive and the EBA Regulation should exclude any role of EDGA in the rescue of distressed banks and banking groups, which would instead be performed by the new supervisory system as will be described.

Finally, as has been made clear by the preceding discussion, a deposit guarantee scheme not supported by a system of early corrective action would be exposed to the risk of regulatory forbearance, so that the fund and the guaranteed deposits would not be effectively and credibly protected. This is why an EU system of mandated corrective action is needed to complete the system: as set out in detail in Chapter 4, the new European Banking Authority should have adequate powers to prevent and manage the crisis of pan-European banks.

---

[40] Bernet & Walter (2009) identified four possible models for deposit guarantee schemes, envisaging increasing powers for the deposit guarantee agency: 1) the 'pay box' model, with functions limited to the payout of covered deposits; 2) the "cost reducer' model, with the task of handling crisis and insolvency of guaranteed institutions with the lowest possible cost and externalities for the financial intermediation system, also with powers to intervene in the guaranteed banks and arrange preventive and corrective measures to protect deposits; 3) the 'resolution facilitator' model, entailing a proactive support of troubled institutions and 4) the 'supervisor' model, with direct supervisory powers. Our proposal is a mix of the pay box and the cost reducer model, since EDGA performs only the payout functions, while it is EBA that plays the "cost reducer" role (see Chapter 4).

[41] An alternative proposal envisages the creation of a Resolution/Stabilisation Fund, charged with crisis management and resolution, participated by EU member states and funded by EU cross-border banks (ABI, 2010).

3. BANK CRISIS RESOLUTION

When serious cracks started to emerge in the financial system, the authorities in the main financial centres were taken by surprise and reacted somewhat erratically. In some cases, they extended government guarantees to some or all creditors; in others, they injected capital into the troubled institutions or took them over outright; and in one case, Lehman Brothers, they let them go bust.

This piecemeal approach is bound to magnify the disruptions to the financial system and the eventual costs to taxpayers, as well epitomized by the Lehman and AIG cases. The chaotic way in which Lehman Brothers was placed into bankruptcy led to uncertainty and contagious disruptions in financial markets, even if Lehman was not a deposit-taking institution, due to great uncertainty on exposures and the probability of recovery. Runs developed on money market funds that were believed to be invested in Lehman commercial paper, rapidly spilling over to corporate commercial paper markets, where liquidity evaporated. Lehman was also a large prime broker for many hedge funds, which lost access to their credit lines and were forced to liquidate their positions, as well as losing access to their collateral placed with Lehman. Bank equity prices fell sharply and the interbank markets collapsed.

The US government took the opposite decision to rescue AIG in order to avoid the disruptions that could derive from failure to honour their CDS liabilities. The initial financial support was $85 billion, but eventually ballooned to almost $200 billion without effectively resolving the situation.[42] Repeated injections of capital eventually adding up to enormous amounts were also a feature of many banking bail-outs in

---

[42] For a detailed review of the measures adopted to stabilize AIG see Baxter (2010).

Europe, the prominent examples being the Royal Bank of Scotland and the German Hypo Real Estate.

Thus public authorities seemed caught between a rock and a hard place, i.e. disorderly failure with unpredictable consequences on one side, and an open-ended injection of public funds on the other. But this is only due to the absence of a special resolution procedure for banks, able to effectively halt the confidence crisis from spreading and at the same time place tight limits on recourse to the public purse. Figure 3.1 shows graphically the two unpleasant outcomes together with a third possibility, which is superior to both, that is available when adequate resolution procedures for banks are in place before crisis strikes.

Figure 3.1 Fiscal cost and systemic impact in resolution regimes

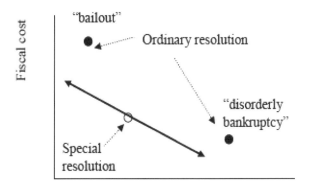

Source: Čihák & Nier (2009).

One additional consequence of the decision to let Lehman Brothers go bust, as has been mentioned, was that the authorities and analysts fell prey to the belief that large financial institutions cannot be allowed to fail. However, accepting that some financial institutions cannot fail must be wrong, since it entails that those financial institutions effectively operate with an open-ended guarantee that governments will intervene to rescue them from their mistakes. A financial system in which all the big financial institutions are guaranteed by the government entails massive moral hazard and is inherently unstable, since the fundamental check on reckless behaviour by bankers and financiers, the danger of going bankrupt, would be eliminated.

The correct conclusion should have been that existing resolution tools were not adequate to avoid or contain systemic spillovers. A fundamental problem in generating destabilising behaviour within the financial system was the lack of a credible threat of bankruptcy for its largest institutions. Building effective resolution procedures that will enable most, if not all, financial institutions to fail without disrupting the financial system becomes a key task in the endeavour to build a more stable financial system. The Damocles sword of 'too-big-to-fail' must be effectively removed from the system.

An effective system to manage banking crises must possess two features: it must be able to keep depositors safe, as well as reassure counterparties in the normal running of business on the continuity of basic functions – of systemic relevance – of the failing financial institution.

In this regard, time is of the essence. The forced sale of assets, under pressure from vanishing supply of funds, may destroy value beyond what is justified by the bank's capital position. This is why ordinary bankruptcy procedures will in general not do: because ordinary procedures, managed by courts, are unable to preserve viable relations with the bank's counterparties, since they typically involve a suspension of all claims on the bank and aim at protecting all creditors without regard to their relevance for the continuing viability of the financial system. Moreover, the formal declaration of insolvency – which at some stage is always required by general bankruptcy procedures – may hamper, rather than favour, rapid redress of troubled financial institutions (Brierley, 2009).

For this reason it is unavoidable to entrust resolution to special administrative procedures managed by banking supervisors, which can ensure the continuity of key banking relations while starting to sort out counterparties' positions and the capital effectively available to meet emerging losses. Their main purpose, as already mentioned, is to protect depositors and key functions with systemic relevance, while all other interests at stake are treated with lower priority: which does not mean that will be totally sacrificed, only that they will be dealt with in a subsequent resolution phase, which may well turn out to provide better value for all parties concerned.

The administrators should be capable of deciding all actions needed to recapitalise the bank and restructure its operations without leaving much room for shareholders or other creditors to interfere. Should all efforts to rescue the bank fail, liquidation procedures should be capable of preserving the continuity of fundamental banking relations with depositors and other key counterparties of systemic importance. When this happens, the performing assets should be conferred to a bridge bank, and the impaired assets should remain with the residual bank, to be subsequently liquidated.

3.1   National frameworks for bank crisis resolution

Most European countries apply ordinary insolvency procedures also to banks (*lex generalis*),[43] albeit often with certain adaptations. Corporate bankruptcy rules primarily aim at protecting all creditors, typically organised in classes of varying priority among which residual values are shared in the liquidation process. Many aspects of bank liquidation – such as the calculation of assets values, verification of claims, attribution of assets – are regulated as in the liquidation of any commercial company.[44]

Ordinary bankruptcy proceedings are managed by judges in court proceedings; bank supervisors normally have limited control over actions taken by the judges and are not entitled to interfere with the aim of preserving financial stability. Court-administered procedures must resolve creditor claims "in an orderly and fair manner" while respecting *par condicio creditorum*: this principle is in direct conflict with providing privileged status to insured depositors.

General bankruptcy laws give the liquidator exclusive control over the assets and liabilities of the failed bank. As noted by Garcia et al. (2009), "by the time a court-administered procedure has commenced, judicial liquidation of a bank is … much more likely than rehabilitation". And indeed experience has repeatedly shown the potentially disruptive effects of applying normal bankruptcy procedures to banking, or bank-like, institutions, due to the destabilising effects of depositors and creditors trying to protect their claims.

For this reason, some countries – e.g. Austria, Belgium, France, Germany and Luxembourg – had already, prior to the recent crisis, introduced special rules into their corporate insolvency law to deal with bank insolvency, notably by reserving the right to file for bankruptcy to

---

[43] Hüpkes (2003).

[44] For a clear description of the legal systems, see IMF & World Bank (2009).

banking supervisors and entrusting them with the management of the procedure.

In particular, in Belgium the Banking, Finance and Insurance Commission has the power to appoint a special commissioner whose consent is necessary for all acts and decisions taken by the decision-making organs within the bank, including the shareholders. All decisions assumed without authorisation of the special commissioner are null and void.

In France, bank liquidation may only be initiated with the opinion of the Commission Bancaire and is supervised by the courts. The Commission Bancaire appoints an official administrator and may obtain a court order for the transfer of bank shares. Liquidation is a proceeding with separate liquidators acting respectively under the control of the Commission Bancaire and the direction of the courts pursuant to the commercial code.

In Germany, the bank insolvency proceedings may only be initiated by the supervisory agency (BaFin) but are conducted under the corporate insolvency law and are overseen by the courts. The legal framework does not provide specific restructuring powers for the supervisory agency such as purchase-and-assumption transactions or bridge banks to facilitate prompt restructuring. A number of simplifications to speed up the procedure were approved in 2009, following the Hypo-Re crisis, with the Act on the further Stabilisation of the Financial Market[45] and the Financial Market Stabilisation Fund Act.[46] The former has provided for special powers to decide the dispossession and transfer of bank shares into public ownership; the latter has simplified the procedures for the acquisition of shares and risk positions of financial institutions by the Stabilisation Fund set up to recapitalise financial institutions.

Few countries, on the other hand, already have a special administrative regime for resolving bank insolvency (*lex specialis*), notably including the United States, with the FDIC resolution powers, and in the European Union, Italy and, as a newcomer, the United Kingdom.[47] Under

---

[45] Enacted on 20 March 2009.

[46] Adopted on 17 October 2009.

[47] The United Kingdom enacted new legislation introducing special procedures once the inadequacy of ordinary bankruptcy rules was exposed by the Northern Rock deposit run and the de facto insolvency of banking giants Royal Bank of Scotland and TSB Lloyds.

these regimes the initiative and responsibility for managing the procedure belong to the banking supervisors, with an only marginal role of the judiciary – typically called upon ex-post to verify that all interested parties were treated fairly.

Under special resolution regimes, the resolution authority gives priority to maintaining depositor confidence and financial stability. Moreover the minimisation of the public costs of resolution is an explicit objective, and for this reason the resolution authority has powers such as that of transferring to a 'bridge bank' under temporary public ownership the par value of insured deposits, and the estimated recovery value of uninsured deposits and credit lines. The recent UK legislative banking reform was influenced by similar considerations.[48]

The involvement of banking supervisors is the key element, because authorities that have inspected the bank since the beginning of its activities until the crisis may be in the best position to estimate rapidly the recovery value of the institution as a whole or in parts. If the bank is to be sold, the immediate estimation and allocation of credit losses is of great importance. Even in a liquidation, supervisors have an informational advantage about the financial condition of the bank and its position as a counterparty to contracts with non-depository institutions.

Under the US procedure, the FDIC has a broad range of options for dealing with a bank failure including liquidation, purchase and assumption transaction with another institution, establishment of a conservatorship, provision of open bank assistance or creation of a bridge bank. A bridge bank is a temporary national bank created by the FDIC to take over and maintain banking services for the customers of a failed bank (Herring, 2003; Bliss & Kaufman 2007). It is designed to fill the gap between the failure of the bank and the final resolution. The limit of this procedure is that its application is limited to depository, FDIC-insured banks. No special regime for bank holding companies and other financial institutions (e.g. investment banks, insurance companies) is provided: in the failure of

---

[48] Kaufman (2004) argues that insolvent banks are resolved efficiently when the sum of their aggregate credit and liquidity losses is at, or close to, zero; Eisenbeis & Kaufman (2006) affirm that the public policy objective of resolving banks should be to reduce costs (both public and private) and permit free entry and exit of failed banks at minimal cost to society.

Lehman Brothers, the ordinary discipline for reorganisation (Chapter 11 of the Bankruptcy Code) was applied. Some reforms to the system are now considered by the US Congress to create a resolution process that could be applied to both banks and non-bank financial institutions, and their holding companies.

In Italy, the 'special administration' is normally commenced by the Minister for the Economy and Finance, by decree, acting on a proposal from the Bank of Italy, and brings the bank under the full control of these administrative authorities.[49] This procedure applies when serious administrative irregularities or violations of laws have lead to sizable capital losses. Special administration may last up to one year, and the Bank of Italy may propose all the needed restructuring measures, including transfer of the bank or part of its assets to another bank. Shareholders are deprived of some of their rights but any restructuring operation is normally subject to their approval. To the extent that no other solution is found, the Ministry for the Economy and Finance, on a proposal from the Bank of Italy, can withdraw the license of the bank and start compulsory liquidation.

In the United Kingdom, a new Banking Act was adopted in 2009; a Code of Conduct then clarified when the authorities can use their new powers and how to deploy them in emergency conditions. Three options are envisaged for the troubled bank: i) the Bank of England has the power to transfer all or part of a bank (either through a share or business sale) to a private sector purchaser;[50] ii) the Bank of England can transfer all or part of the bank (through a business sale) to a bridge bank owned and operated by the Bank of England; and iii) the Treasury can transfer the shares of a bank to a nominee or a company wholly owned by the Treasury.[51]

---

[49] A request to place the bank in special administration may also be addressed by the governing board of the bank or an extraordinary general meeting of shareholders.

[50] It is a purely administrative action; in fact, there is no court involvement and no need to wait until a breach of a threshold condition has occurred. In practice it is possible for a bank that is still balance sheet solvent to be the subject of the special resolution tool.

[51] This tool is meant to be used only if the others tools available to the Bank of England have already been fully explored and found not appropriate. In particular

In case of partial transfer of assets and liabilities to a commercial purchaser or a bridge bank, some assets and liabilities will remain with the 'residual bank' under administration. The procedure will try to rescue the residual bank as a going concern or, at any event, to achieve the best feasible outcome for creditors. The Bank of England plays the central role in the procedure since its agreement must be obtained by the administrator in the decisions to set up the residual bank – performing de facto the functions played in ordinary bankruptcy proceedings by the committee of creditors.

In case of insolvency, a special court-based liquidation develops whose primary objective is to ensure that depositors with eligible claims under the Financial Services Compensation Scheme (FSCS) are paid promptly. The Bank of England, the FSA and the Treasury are all entitled to ask the court for a bank insolvency order; if the court finds that appropriate conditions are verified,[52] she will issue a winding up order and appoint a liquidator. This procedure is only available for banks that have depositors with claims eligible for compensation from the FSCS.

As has been described, while some countries have a specific resolution regime for banks, others apply the ordinary corporate insolvency law. An effective cross-border resolution is all but impossible if the tools available under national law are not only different, but also mutually incompatible. For example if in one country an administrative authority has the power to transfer assets to a private buyer, while this is forbidden in a second country where only a judge could authorise it, a prompt common intervention by those two authorities to deal with affiliated banks in their jurisdictions just cannot happen.

As a consequence of their heterogeneous legal frameworks, in the recent crisis countries have tried to ring-fence national assets of cross-border groups and have applied national resolution measures at national level, rather than look for group solution. Ring-fencing local assets within a cross-border group may amplify the problem, rather than resolve it. The

---

it can only be used to protect the public interest and resolve or reduce a serious threat to the stability of the financial system.

[52] Ground A: a bank is unable, or likely to become unable, to pay its debts; ground B: a winding up would be in the public interest; ground C: the winding up would be fair (Section 96(1) Insolvency Act 2009).

incentives for the states to coordinate and renounce to ring-fencing are strongly limited by their legal duty to protect the national stakeholders' interests (see Box 3.1 below on ring-fencing).

Box 3.1 Ring-fencing in bank crisis resolution

It is by now a commonplace that banks grow internationally but die nationally. Inter-country cooperation between financial supervisors deteriorates rapidly in crisis conditions, basically owing to incentive conflicts between national authorities, which typically try to protect home operators, often at the expense of creditors and stakeholders in the countries hosting the foreign branches and subsidiaries of the banking group.*

In this context, countries willing to host large foreign banking groups tend to require them to obtain a separate banking license in the country and set up a separate legal entity, a subsidiary, with adequate own capital and subject to full supervision by the host country. Should the parent company threaten to become insolvent, the natural response of local authorities is to try to 'ring- fence' local operations and, if need be, seize local assets of the bank in order to protect its local creditors and other stakeholders. The Fortis collapse provides a clear example.

On the positive side, the working group of the Committee of Basel Supervisors on Cross-Border Bank Resolution (CBRG) in its 2009 Report (BCBS, 2009b) has noted that effective ring-fencing and a territorial approach to crisis resolution can facilitate early corrective action by local authorities and ensure that local assets of the local branch exceed local liabilities. Moreover, the danger of separate resolution under local control puts pressure on the home jurisdiction of the parent company to share information and tackle decisively the problems besetting the institution. Ring-fencing can also contribute to the resiliency of the separate operations within host countries by encouraging the separate functionality of the local operating branch. Ring-fencing has occurred even where there were agreements between national jurisdictions providing for the allocation of responsibility for deposit insurance. For the host jurisdictions, ring-fencing is also attractive since it allows greater control on capital, liquidity and risk management of locally established banks; however, this kind of control can also impose costs on the host jurisdiction if cross-border institutions limit or reduce their operations in that country as a result.

More generally, the host-country authorities will have great difficulties in obtaining full information on the conditions of the parent bank from the home-country primary supervisor. Ring-fencing may not be sufficient to avoid the collapse of the local subsidiary and may well lead to a worse outcome for local creditors; it may also complicate the efforts to resolve the bank crisis short of liquidation (Krimminger, 2005), locally and for the whole group.

The parent bank and the home-country authorities, on their part, may be concerned by the potentially adverse repercussions of ring-fencing in a crisis, with local losses spilling over to endanger the entire group. Indeed, ring-fencing can also aggravate the difficulties of the group as a whole because of the resulting segregation of internal funding and liquidity flows. It may hamper orderly resolution by the home authorities on a consolidated basis by reducing the pool of assets available for intra-group transfer in order to meet emerging losses.

The recent crisis has also demonstrated that in a period of market instability there is little time to bring about cooperative cross-border agreements in managing bank crises. One noteworthy exception has been the agreement brokered by the IMF, together with the European Commission, between some Eastern European countries and major foreign banking groups active in those countries to recapitalise their subsidiaries and maintain credit flows. Significantly, capital requirements were determined with reference to local deposit collection.**

In general, lacking an agreement between home and host jurisdictions on burden-sharing in case of crisis and resolution, national authorities are likely to fall back to territorial "ring-fenced" resolution. And indeed many national supervisors, notably including the British FSA, are making explicit their intention to do just that. The Basel CBRG has recommended a "middle ground" approach envisaging ring-fencing of systemically important functions performed by the bank, rather than the local legal entities. In their view this approach would limit moral hazard and promote market discipline by shifting a greater share of losses onto shareholders and other creditors. In fact, as noted by Hüpkes (2004), ring-fencing can operate as a particular form of detachment or ex-post separation of certain functions, regardless of their placement in branches or subsidiaries. This approach would require appropriate changes to national laws so as to facilitate continuity of key financial functions across nations.

---

* For a clear description of the agency problem, see Eisenbeis & Kaufman (2006).
** See for example European Commission & IMF (2009).

3.2   Ingredients of an effective resolution regime

It is now broadly agreed that in order to preserve financial stability and minimise the cost of bank crises, all countries should establish effective resolution procedures and that these procedures should be managed by banking supervisory authorities endowed with special powers rather than by judges in court. Special problems arise for cross-border banking groups that require supranational arrangements.

In their recent report (BCBS, 2009b), the special working group of the Committee of Basel Supervisors on cross-border bank resolution has listed the key ingredients that all resolution procedures should possess at national level in order to be effective. They notably include adequate administrative powers to deal with all types of financial institutions in difficulties (for a review of the main tools, see Box 3.2). National resolution authorities should also have legal authority to delay temporarily the operation of contractual termination clauses in order to complete the transfer of the contract to other entities or promote the continuity of market functions. And they are encouraged more in general to use risk mitigation techniques to enhance the resiliency of critical financial or market functions, e.g. enforceable netting arrangements, collateralisation and segregation of client positions. This end would be notably helped by encouraging the migration of derivative contracts to organised clearing platforms with central counterparty.

The Basel Supervisors also recommend the creation of a national framework to coordinate the resolution of legal entities of financial groups and financial conglomerates within each jurisdiction. The absence of a procedure for the coordinated resolution of the companies in a financial group limits the possibilities available to national authorities for crisis management and poses limits to the possible coordinated resolution of such cross-border groups. While other issues, such as the lack of time or inadequate information, may render any reorganising process complex, the absence of a coordinated resolution mechanism for the firms in financial groups may mean that the only alternative is a disorderly collapse or a bail-out.

In this connection, the Basel working group refers to the recommendations developed by UNCITRAL for the improvement of national group insolvency proceedings (to be finally adopted in 2010), which include the possibility of joint application and procedural coordination of proceedings of different legal entities in a group, intra-group guarantees after insolvency proceedings have commenced, appointment of a single administrator, implementation of a joint reorganisation plan, extension of liability, or substantive consolidation (pooling of assets).[53]

Two further recommendations concern the reduction of complexity and advance planning for orderly resolution by the banks or financial conglomerate themselves. It is recommended that supervisors work closely with the management of financial groups to understand how group structures would be resolved in a crisis and, when they believe that these structures are too complex to permit an orderly resolution, they should encourage a reduction in complexity through regulatory and prudential requirements. In addition, all institutions of systemic relevance should be required to draw a contingency plan, "proportionate to the size and complexity of the institution", to facilitate the rapid resolution or winding down in case of need. Such contingency plans should become a regular component of supervisory oversight.

Quite a few supervisory authorities and the Financial Stability Board (FSB, 2009) have now specifically endorsed these recommendations, which are likely to be adopted in the coming months. While they remain controversial within the financial community, they clearly offer a better alternative to straight regulatory interventions to modify the structure of financial conglomerates, as some governments are now starting to see as the sole viable solution.

Specific recommendations concern the supranational coordination of resolution proceedings. First of all, it is necessary that the different national authorities develop a clear understanding of respective responsibilities for supervision, liquidity provision, crisis management and resolution. They are encouraged to develop arrangements that allow for the timely and effective sharing of information both during the normal course of supervisory activities and on the occasion of crises. The Basel CBRG also recommends that, in order to promote better coordination among national authorities in cross-border resolutions, national authorities should consider

---

[53] For a clear and complete description of the UNCITRAL Legislative Guide on Insolvency Law, see Panzani (2009).

the development of procedures to facilitate the mutual recognition of crisis management and resolution measures.[54]

While representing considerable progress relative to the present situation, these recommendations do not resolve the critical issue of unitary management of resolution procedures for cross-border banks and financial conglomerates.

Box 3.2 Special resolution tools

Acquisition by a private sector purchaser. When a financial institution is under stress, the desirable solution often is the sale of the institution as a whole to a strong private purchaser, ensuring continuity of services and ample protection of the interests of creditors and counterparties. To this end, the resolution authority needs to have power to conclude a private sale without the consent of shareholders, even if the sale conditions entail losses for them.

Assisted sale to a private sector purchaser. If the assets of the bank are difficult to value, the authorities can assist with a guarantee to the purchaser. Such a guarantee does not extend to shareholders or creditors, and therefore reduces moral hazard and preserves incentives for prudent risk management.

Bridge bank. The bank is split in two parts: a new licensed bank under the control of the banking authority to carry on the performing assets, including some or all of the deposits and other liabilities. The impaired assets and remaining portion of liabilities stay with the residual bank, which is subsequently closed and liquidated. If reorganisation of the bank fails, this technique allows operations to continue in the bridge bank, while the residual bank can be stripped of its charter and liquidated.

Partial transfer of assets, deposits and liabilities to a 'good bank'. When some of the bank's assets are doubtful, non-performing or difficult to value and it is difficult to find a buyer, the authority needs to have power to split the institution into two parts: a good part within easy-to-value or 'clean' assets and deposits, and a residual institution that will keep in its books all of the assets difficult to value or illiquid.

---

[54] UNCITRAL has adopted, on 1 July 2009, a Practice Guide on Cross-Border Insolvency Cooperation (UNCITRAL, 2009). The aim of the Guide is not to give any recommendation but to provide judges and stakeholders with information on existing practices in insolvency proceedings for cross-border coordination and cooperation.

Temporary public control. As a last remedy, the government should have the power to take temporary public control (nationalisation) of the failing institution. This tool may be most appropriate where a significant amount of public funds are necessary to stabilise the failing institution, for example if the banking system is highly concentrated and there are few possibilities for a sale to a private purchaser.

*Specific tools for banks' systemic functions.** Banks and financial institutions perform some key systemic functions whose interruption might impair the good functioning of the financial system and eventually undermine financial stability. For this reason systemically relevant functions deserve particular protection. The preservation of their integrity and continuity can be obtained through the following specific tools:

a. the *replacement* of the failing institution as provider of systemically relevant functions to other financial intermediaries can reduce the impact of failure. The possibility to find an alternative provider depends on the nature of the function; it can work effectively for trading in securities, foreign exchange, money market instruments and deposit-taking. To find a replacement, one must consider the availability of alternative suppliers and the necessary infrastructure to exercise the function;

b. the *detachment* of systemically relevant functions consists of insulating the function from the winding down and permitting the performance of the function without disruption. The feasibility of detachment will depend on a number of factors, such as separability and transferability of the function and legal certainty. To facilitate resort to this tool, the authorities must consider developing contingency plans, including functions ring-fencing, which may help in realising the scope of this instrument by attaching strict conditions previously accepted by creditors. A statutory procedure to realise the detachment is the bridge bank;

c. the *immunisation* of the systemically relevant functions from failure may be achieved by collateralisation of counterparty claims, netting by reducing counterparty exposures from gross amounts to net values, carve-outs by statutory law or contractual agreements from insolvency law, and market structure measures providing strict rules of antitrust. Collateralisation and netting are commonly used to strengthen the financial infrastructure, such as the payments, clearing and settlement systems. A certain degree of immunisation can be achieved through statutory and contractual mechanisms.

---

* Hüpkes (2004).

3.3   Legal hurdles in special resolution regimes

A critical feature in a special resolution regime is the balancing of the wide public interest to a solution that minimises systemic damage with the interests of private shareholders. Under existing legal systems, shareholders are only liable for any of the debts of the company up to the value of their capital stake. However, even when capital is largely or wholly depleted, their property rights confer upon them the right of ordinary and extraordinary decisions on company operations and activities. Special protections of property rights may be present in legal and even constitutional rules. Therefore, care is needed to ensure that actions that may be adopted under special resolution procedures either do not infringe these shareholders' rights or do so under appropriate exemptions from existing legal arrangements (Box 3.3).

Box 3.3 Possible limitations of shareholders' rights*

Pre-packaged resolution. Authorities could require financial institutions to come to a private solution, instead of using their statutory resolution powers. Such agreements could set out contingency plans for circumstances in which the institution becomes financially troubled, including reorganisation measures, and a corporate structure that would facilitate a wind-down. For example, the bank's shareholders could approve a resolution giving the board power to bring in new investors rapidly without their approval. This option could be especially valuable for complex group structures in a cross-border context. The pre-packaged resolution would of course need to be drawn up in consultation with all relevant national supervisors. It should be noted, however, that such contractual arrangements can only be effective for early resolution, for afterwards they could be superseded by action under the insolvency law. For this reason, a pre-packaged solution is not a substitute for a statutory resolution regime.

   Layering bank liabilities. An appropriate structuring of banks' liabilities would also facilitate private resolution of bank crises, and make the creation of a bridge bank workable. One suggestion that should be considered in this context is to require banks to issue minimum proportions to own capital of subordinated debt, convertible into equity when capital falls below or the CDS spread rises above certain pre-defined thresholds (Calomiris, 2000; Kay, 2009). The rationale is straightforward: the market will place a price on these issues that will be based on the estimated probability of conversion; and conversion will mean that bond-holders will share the risk of losing their investment, if the bank were to become

---

insolvent, and shareholders will be diluted. Therefore, bond-holders would have a strong incentive to monitor the bank managers; and the latter would have a strong incentive to manage prudently, so as to obtain a low interest on their convertible bonds. Market discipline would thereby be strengthened. Achim Dübel has suggested that in general a tiered structure of bank (subordinated) liabilities would in practice be equivalent to pre-packaged resolution.

Temporary suspension of shareholders' rights. A temporary suspension of shareholders' rights to decide changes in the bank's capital structure could be provided by law in order to favour quick resolution of bank crises. A good example are the rules introduced in Germany in 2009 permitting to raise equity capital without a shareholder resolution and excluding subscription by existing shareholders.

Shareholders' divestiture. An extreme measure, provided by law, could be the total divestiture of shareholders in case of certain conditions. The bank and all its assets would be transferred to a trustee or receiver. This procedure would be a form of compulsory administration that ends the existence of the firm as a legal entity and extinguishes the shareholders' rights. However, if the bank still has positive net worth, shareholders should be paid an adequate compensation, which could consist of a monetary payment or take other forms that would give the former shareholders a claim on the future earnings of the bank.

Source: Hüpkes (2009a).

In fair weather the room for conflict between the shareholders' interest in increasing the value of their shares and the depositors' interest in making sure that their money is safe, typically is small – and in the main is taken care of by prudential rules. Conversely, in a crisis situation, shareholders' interests may be in sharp contrast with those of depositors and the wider public. For instance, while depositors may want substantial injections of fresh capital, this would dilute shareholders, who are likely to resist. Actions needed to preserve the continuity of critical functions of an insolvent bank may well prejudice shareholders' interest in maintaining the unity of the business. If decisions are subject to the approval of shareholders, the needed actions may never be undertaken, to the greater damage of depositors and financial stability at large.

For this reason, many national resolution regimes contain provisions that suspend or limit shareholder rights. These measures can have various level of intrusiveness. Some suspend certain governance rights for a limited period, others have a deeper impact on shareholders.

For instance, in Belgium, the Banking, Finance and Insurance Commission can nominate a special inspector with extended powers to act. In France, the temporary administrator has full powers to administer and represent the institution. The German supervisory authority may suspend current management and appoint a temporary administrator but this leaves shareholder rights nearly unchanged. In Italy, when special administration is started the functions of the general meeting of shareholders are suspended.

In all these cases, the decisions relating to the capital structure remain within the competence of the shareholder meeting and require their support. As a consequence, restructuring measures would always need to be negotiated with shareholders. The notable exception is in the new UK Banking Act, which empowers the authorities to act without the consent of the shareholders.

The content and scope of shareholder rights depend on legal traditions. Shareholder rights are more strongly founded in civil law in Europe than the US. US law requires the general meeting to approve only some decisions and leaves the division of powers up to the company; as a consequence, the board holds all powers that are not explicitly reserved to shareholders.

Under corporate law in most European countries, the shareholder meeting has all the powers not attributed by law to the board. Usually the firm charter or a shareholder resolution cannot assign to the board powers that are attributed to the shareholder meeting by the law. Shareholders must vote on various decisions relevant for crisis resolution, such as spin-offs and divisions, the increase or decrease of company capital, and the waiver of pre-emptive rights associated with an increase in capital funded by outside investors.

The hurdles created by this approach came into sharp evidence in the Fortis case, when Belgian shareholders objected to the government's decision to sell the group's activities to BNP Paribas and brought the case before the Belgian Commercial Court, maintaining that the sale required shareholder approval even if it had already been decided by contract. The Court of First Instance ruled that approval by shareholders was unnecessary; but the Court of Appeal decided the opposite and ordered a shareholders' vote. The shareholders voted unanimously against the sale, which was then renegotiated with the Belgian State and BNP, and was approved by a subsequent new meeting of shareholders.

Quite the opposite happened in the United States when Bear Stearns was acquired by JPMorgan Chase, and the structure of the contract explicitly excluded refusal by shareholders. In the AIG case the government was handed preferred stock issued without shareholder agreement under the New York Stock Exchange's Shareholder Approval Policy.[55]

The Commission Communication on Crisis Management in the Banking Sector (European Commission, 2009) explicitly raises the possibility of adjusting Company Law Directives to balance shareholder rights with public interest so as to facilitate speedy interventions by the authorities to restructure a failing institution. The Second Company Law Directive (77/91/EEC) contains provisions mandating shareholder approval for any increase or reduction of capital as well as rules on shareholder pre-emption rights, which indeed may hinder or impede administrative resolution of an ailing bank. The Shareholders' Rights Directive (2007/36/EC) requires long leads for calling shareholder meetings which may slow down resolution decisions.

Another potential obstacle for effective administrative resolution of a failing bank is represented by legal actions by affected parties against the banking authorities' measures. Decisions taken by the banking authorities in the framework of insolvency proceedings are often challenged in court by shareholders or creditors, notably regarding the decision to commence insolvency proceedings or specific actions undertaken during the proceedings that may prejudice some interests. Even if banking authorities must be accountable for their actions, and the affected parties need to be legally protected, it is important to ensure that such actions do not undermine the efficiency of the insolvency procedures of the bank. Accordingly, the legal framework must specify the circumstances in which such challenges are legitimate and the remedies that affected parties may seek, in view of the need to preserve the certainty and credibility of the banking authorities' decisions.

---

[55] The preferred stock was issued without shareholder approval in application of an exception that can be invoked when the delay necessary to secure approval by shareholders would endanger the financial stability of the company.

Legal action against decisions in insolvency proceedings may actually consist of: i) judicial review of the banking authorities' actions assumed in the context of insolvency procedures and ii) legal action to obtain compensation from the banking authorities or their representatives, for damage caused by specific measures in the context of insolvency proceedings.

Judicial review of the banking authorities' decisions. In most countries the administrative law provides for court review of the measures taken by an administrative authority. The court will overturn their decision when the action is found to have exceeded legal authority. It is important to specify that the courts should not be able to stop resolution by the administrative authorities, but only review the legality of the procedure *post factum.* The review should not extend to the use of discretionary powers, except in case of manifestly gross mistake or abuse of power. In general, the court should not be allowed to substitute its own views for those of the administrative authority charged with managing the procedure.

Court reviews should be conducted rapidly and should not block the resolution proceedings. Where the actions of the banking authorities inflict damages on shareholders or other interested parties without adequate justification and it is impossible to restore the previous situation, the only effective remedy is compensation for damage; but legal rules may even allow for a close circumscription of the circumstances in which damages may be awarded.

Actions for damages against the banking authorities. Parties affected by the actions of the banking authorities in insolvency proceedings may also file a lawsuit for damages resulting directly from the banking authorities' behaviour, as a consequence of 'improper' conduct in exercising their powers. Most countries limit this kind of liability only to cases of negligence or bad faith. Again, a clear legal framework in such cases is essential for the effective functioning of resolution procedures.

3.4 European legal instruments for cross-border banking groups

The introduction of special resolution regimes based on common principles in all the member states, as advocated by BIS supervisors and as has been described, would greatly improve the situation but would not suffice for cross-border banking groups. The recent crisis has once again shown the need for a special framework applicable to large cross-border financial institutions.

Large cross-border financial institutions are typically organised as groups with branches and subsidiaries, often with very complex structures.[56] The parent can be itself an operating firm or a holding company. Branches are not separate legal entities but simply operative extensions of the parent bank, which remains fully responsible for their liabilities. Subsidiaries, on the other hand, are separate legal entities with their own capital and company organisation. They are connected to the head company through complex ownership structures, which determine how the different entities are run and who is responsible for their liabilities; often, they are also connected to the head company and other entities in the group by myriad credit and other business relations.[57]

The main issue here arises from the fact that legal structures – which are decided for legal, accounting, tax and other considerations – often do not reflect the real functional organisation and decision-taking (Hüpkes, 2009b). Typically, IT systems, liquidity management, risk control and other key functions are fully centralised: centralisation and integration of key functions bring considerable benefits but may blur the understanding on the part of the board, auditors and market analysts of the group's actual risk and financial position. For this reason, sometimes host countries impose burdensome restrictions on branches because of their limited power over them in supervision and crisis resolution (Cerutti et al., 2005).

Thus, the real problem of large cross-border financial institutions is their complexity and lack of correspondence of legal and functional structures. Both factors greatly complicate the allocation of assets and losses in a crisis and make it close to impossible to implement a quick and orderly reorganisation or wind-down.

There are two approaches to managing the crisis of a cross-border financial institution with subsidiaries and branches in different jurisdictions: the universal and the territorial approach.

---

[56] See Herring & Carmassi (2010) for a detailed analysis of corporate structures of large and complex financial institutions and the implications for financial stability.

[57] Lehman Brothers was composed by more than 2,000 separate legal entities with intricate legal and economic relationships.

Under the universal approach, the resolution is based on the law of the country where the insolvent institution has its parent firm. The decisions of the resolution authority in the principal jurisdiction are applied to all the companies of the insolvent group, including those located in foreign jurisdictions.

Under the territorial approach each country applies its own law to companies placed in its jurisdiction so that each insolvent branch or subsidiary is governed by local insolvency law. It requires a declaration of insolvency in each country where the insolvent firm maintains operating units.

Within the European Union, the Directive 2001/24/EC[58] embraces the principle of universality for branches but not subsidiaries. Moreover, the directive does not try to harmonise national legislation on reorganisation and winding up of credit institutions. It establishes that any reorganisation or winding up of a credit institution with branches in different states must be initiated and carried out under a single procedure, by the competent authority of the home country of the parent company, and that the effects of these measures must be mutually recognised. Subsidiaries in foreign jurisdictions are not covered by the directive. Moreover the directive contains a number of conflict-of-law rules applicable to set-offs, property rights, netting and repurchase agreements.[59]

---

[58] Directive 2001/24/EC of the European Parliament and of the Council on the reorganisation and winding up for credit institutions.

[59] In particular, under Article 10(2)(c), the law of the home member state shall determine the conditions under which set-offs may be invoked. Under Article 23 of the Directive "the adoption of reorganisation measures or the opening of winding up proceedings shall not affect the right of creditors to demand the set-off of their claims against the claims of the credit institution, where such a set-off is permitted by the law applicable to the credit institution's claim". This provision "shall not preclude the actions for voidness, voidability or unenforceability of legal acts detrimental to all creditors". Article 24 of the Directive establishes that "the enforcement of proprietary rights in instruments or other rights in such instruments the existence or transfer of which presupposes their recording in a register, an account or a centralized deposit system held or located in a Member State shall be governed by the law of the Member State where the register, account, or centralized deposit system in which those rights are recorded is held or located". Article 25 provides that "netting agreements shall be governed solely by the law of the contract which governs such agreements". Without prejudice to the

Finally the Winding Up Directive provides procedural rules only with reference to each legal entity within a cross-border banking group.

This limited field of application does not take into account synergies within a group which may be in the interest of creditors in case of restructuring. A group-based approach to winding up and reorganisation can foster survival of subsidiaries and even the entire group by facilitating asset transfers and the unitary resolution of claims and counterparty positions.[60]

However, subsidiaries constitute the principal legal form of European cross-border banks, holding assets of almost €4.6 trillion; subsidiaries of third countries' credit institutions in Europe hold assets of about €1.3 trillion (ECB, 2010). In the absence of a group-based EU legal framework, their crises would be managed locally under host country law, even if in reality those subsidiaries are not self-standing autonomous units. As a consequence, host countries intervene to impose capital and other requirements on the subsidiaries under their control: but these measures would not preserve the subsidiaries from failure, should the parent company go under. The perception that their destiny depends on the parent company would thus make it impossible for the host country to impede a confidence crisis, or a run on its banks, as a result of events unfolding out of its jurisdiction and effective control.

---

above-referenced Article 24, "repurchase agreements shall be governed solely by the law of the contract which governs such agreements" (Article 26), and "transactions carried out in the context of a regulated market shall be governed solely by the law of the contract which governs such transactions"(Article 27). The provisions about set-off and netting should be read in conjunction with Articles 1, 2 and 7 of Directive 2002/47/EC of the European Parliament and of the Council of 6 June 2002 on financial collateral arrangements (Financial Collateral Directive), which requires member states to ensure that a close-out netting provision of a financial collateral arrangement (or an arrangement of which a financial collateral arrangement forms part) to which, inter alia, a credit institution is party can take effect in accordance with its terms notwithstanding the commencement or continuation of winding up proceedings or reorganisation measures in respect of the credit institution.

[60] Very few countries (e.g. Italy) have specific rules for reorganisation and winding up proceedings dedicated to banking groups.

3.5 A new EU framework for reorganisation of cross-border banking groups

The reorganisation of a cross-border banking group involves the application of resolution measures to group entities located in different jurisdictions. To realise a group-based approach, a common framework for coordinated action by the national authorities is needed, based not only on common tools in the member states but also agreed principles for the coordination of all actors and actions affecting the financial group (Hüpkes, 2009c).[61]

In principle, such a European solution can take two forms: fully consolidated resolution for all the entities in a group by the authority of the home country of the parent company, with appropriate arrangements for the delegation of powers by the countries hosting subsidiaries; or a fully centralised procedure under new legal powers entrusted to a new body created by EU legislation. We will argue that the best way to go is a pragmatic combination of elements of the two approaches, keeping to a minimum required changes in existing arrangements and building upon the recent Commission proposal for the reform of supervision.

In their recent consultation paper on the issue, the European Commission has recognised the need for a common framework "that will in future enable authorities to stabilize and control the systemic impact of failing cross-border institutions" (European Commission, 2009), but has not indicated which way to go. It has however put forth some common principles that broadly follow those of the BIS supervisors. In particular, it has stressed the need for all national supervisors to have adequate tools to identify problems in banks at a sufficiently early stage and intervene decisively to restore the health of the institution or wind it down. It has also underlined the importance of limiting the fall-out from failure of a cross-border bank on other banks and the financial system as a whole, among other things by finding solutions to the inconsistencies arising from territorial- separate entity approach to insolvency. And it has advocated the

---

[61] For a proposal of a collegial approach to bank resolution, see Mayes et al. (2007) and Garcia et al. (2009).

establishment of appropriate arrangements to share the fiscal cost of resolution.[62]

In fact, all the elements of a solution at the EU level are there; they only need to be picked up and brought together. As already explained crisis prevention, reorganisation and liquidation would all be part of a resolution procedure managed for each banking group in all countries by the parent administrative authority with adequate powers.

The first step of resolution should be early mandated action by bank supervisors ensuring that, as capital falls below certain thresholds, the bank or banking group will be promptly and adequately recapitalised (as discussed in Chapter 4). If capital continues to fall national supervisors should have the power to intervene and impose reorganisation measures.

While full harmonisation of national laws is clearly not feasible, a revised Reorganisation and Winding Up (framework) Directive could require the member states to adapt their legal system by introducing the required common resolution tools and resolving the legal hurdles that have been described (Box 3.2).[63]

Moreover, as recommended even by the Basel Supervisors (BCBS, 2009b), the new Directive should require the member states to establish a national framework for the resolution of legal entities of financial groups and financial conglomerates within each jurisdiction. The absence of a coordinated resolution mechanism for firms that are part of financial groups may entail that the only alternative is a disorderly collapse or a bail-out.[64] In this connection, policy-makers should take into consideration the

---

[62] The Commission staff working document, accompanying the Communication on the cross-border crisis-management in banking sector, focuses on the impact assessment and takes into consideration all the aspects of these problems.

[63] For the introduction of "A resolution mechanism for financial institutions", see also the Recommendation 16 of "Financial Reform. A framework for financial stability" by the Group of Thirty (G-30, 2009).

[64] Italian legislation already contains a definition of banking group; in particular Article 60 of the 1993 Banking Law provides: "A banking group shall be composed of either of the following: a) an Italian parent bank and the banking, financial and instrumental companies it controls; b) an Italian parent financial company and the banking, financial and instrumental companies it controls, where such companies include at least one bank and the banking and financial companies are of decisive

recommendations developed by UNCITRAL for the improvement of national group insolvency proceedings.[65]

In this spirit, a further modification of the Winding Up Directive should extend the 'universal' principle of resolution of cross-border banking groups not only to branches, but also subsidiaries that, besides not enjoying managerial autonomy, cannot effectively stand alone in case of default. Full universality across both branches and subsidiaries would better reflect the reality of integrated businesses; it would correspond to the already established principle of consolidated group supervision; it is essential in order to create an integrated system of deposit guarantee and mandated action for reorganisation and winding up.[66]

The key principle is that subsidiaries that do not constitute autonomous entities, and therefore could not overcome on their own the failure of the parent bank, should be treated as branches when the institution has to be rescued under the EU system of mandated corrective action or dissolved. In other words, subsidiaries that are de facto branches should be treated as such also in case of insolvency, as they are in the normal conduct of business of the bank when things go well. Separate resolution of subsidiaries would only be allowed to the extent that they would be really independent of the parent company, would be unaffected by the group's liquidation and would not cause danger to the group's survival in case the subsidiary were wound up. In this way, economic function and legal form could be reconciled; the incentives to maintain and operate a complex structure without functional justification would be greatly reduced.

---

importance, as established by the Bank of Italy in compliance with the resolutions of the Credit Committee."

[65] See Chapter 3, Paragraph 3.2.

[66] Garcia et al. (2009) consider that it would also be necessary to agree on a common definition of insolvency. While this would obviously be of help to mark the beginning of liquidation, it is not always strictly necessary under a system – like the one existing in Italy – whereby the administrative resolution authority doesn't need to formalize the existence of a situation of insolvency in order to restructure or sell in pieces a failing institution.

3.6 A new EU liquidation framework for cross-border banking groups

Consistent with the framework that has been developed for the resolution of cross-border banking groups within the EU, when the reorganisation of the bank or group in crisis fails, a bridge bank should be created to ensure continuity of 'sound' banking operations. In that precise moment the residual bank, stripped of its banking charter, should enter liquidation; from that moment onwards all residual rights of creditors and shareholders may be claimed only against the residual bank – whose assets will include the price paid for the assets transferred to the bridge bank. An administrator, appointed by the banking supervisors in charge of the reorganisation, should then take full legal control of the residual bank and manage the liquidation in front of eligible national courts, in accordance with the principle of equal treatment and applicable rules on claim priority.

In order to implement these principles, it is necessary to amend the Winding Up Directive to include the procedures for the creation of the bridge bank and hence the start of liquidation, the criteria and safeguards for the transfer of assets and claims to the bridge bank, the immediate withdrawal of the banking licence for the residual bank, and the duties of the administrator in charge of the liquidation. The administrator should be appointed by the EBA based on a proposal by the College of supervisors.

The primary purpose of the liquidation would be to preserve and optimise the residual bank assets for the satisfaction of creditors, and residual claims by shareholders. Accordingly, the liquidation discipline should include rules for: a suspension of all the claims against the bank ('moratorium'); the sale of the assets in an orderly and cost-effective manner; the distribution of the income to the various classes of creditors in an equitable and transparent manner, in respect of their priority; the immediate enforceability of close-out netting and collateral arrangements relating to financial transactions.

Local courts will remain charged with claims of local creditors and will resolve them on the basis of the local jurisdiction. The UNCITRAL's Practice Guide on Cross-Border Insolvency Cooperation already provides an effective framework for court collaboration.[67]

---

[67] The Guide discusses cooperation in cross-border cases and is based upon a description of experience and practice. Even the "Guidelines applicable to Court-

3.7 Living wills

In order to make resolution possible with limited repercussions on systemic stability, all European banking groups would be required to prepare and regularly update a document detailing the full consolidated structure of legal entities that depend on the parent company for their survival, and a clear description of operational – as distinct from legal – responsibilities and decision-making, notably regarding functions centralised with the parent company.

The document should also include contingency plans describing possible recovery and winding up arrangements, also updated on an ongoing basis, taking account of key factors such as size, interconnectedness, complexity and dependencies (see BCBS, 2009b).[68] Reorganisation and winding up arrangements should be conceived as a menu of options covering such things as: all the claims on the bank and their order of priority; possible segregation arrangements of certain functions to be maintained in case of resolution; ex- ante commitments to conversion of contingent capital into common equity; powers of management to bring in new investors quickly with no need of shareholders' approval; indication of which assets or divisions or subsidiaries might be sold to third parties in case of distress; group-wide contingency funding plan; the management strategy to de-risk the bank business in a short time and to deal with the failure of their largest counterparties (FSA, 2009b).

The document should be made available to supervisors and the EBA, but not to the broad public. This information disclosure requirement would be part of the deposit guarantee contract that cross-border banks covered by the EU deposit guarantee scheme would need to sign with the new European Deposit Guarantee Agency (see Chapter 2 and Chapter 4).

In preparing their living wills, banks would remain fully free to decide the structure and organisation of their business, notably regarding the decision to set up branches or subsidiaries in the foreign jurisdictions where they operate. A legal structure that would greatly facilitate

---

to-Court communications in cross-border cases", adopted in June 2001 by the American Law Institute in association with the International Insolvency Institute, can provide further guidance to create a cooperation framework.

[68] On the role of living wills as catalyst for action, see Avgouleas et al. (2010).

consolidated resolution is offered by the European Company (*Societas Europea*). The SE is a public-limited liability corporation, regulated partly by EU law[69] and partly by the law of the member state, which allows a cross-border group to operate throughout the Union as a unitary group organised with a parent company and operational branches.[70]

Even if this kind of *ex-ante* planning remains controversial within the financial community,[71] it must be remembered that a number of regulatory authorities in the EU have already decided to impose such obligation on banks under their jurisdiction, notably including the UK Financial Services Authority (FSA, 2009b).[72] A recommendation to move in this direction has also been adopted by the Financial Stability Board (FSB, 2009 and FSF, 2009).

Improved disclosure through living wills would contribute to tackle the opacity of banks corporate structures, whose complexity might hamper effective supervision and resolution. The misalignment between legal forms and economic functions makes it extremely difficult for supervisors

---

[69] The *Societas Europea* (SE) is regulated by the Regulation 2001/2157/EC and the Directive 2001/86/EC.

[70] See Dermine (2006) for a full analysis of the decision to expand banking activity abroad through branches or subsidiaries as against through the creation of a European Company (*Societas Europea,* SE) and a review of the case of the Scandinavian bank Nordea, which is not a SE yet because of financial stability and tax reasons.

[71] As affirmed by Ackermann (2009a), "detailed 'living wills' … that outline elaborate winding-down scenarios would not only be very theoretical, but would also lead to inefficient corporate structures that create trapped pools of capital".

[72] Under legislation now before Parliament, the FSA will require banks to compile two distinct documents: the recovery plan and the resolution plan. The first one will set out the firm's plan to respond to severe distress and should contain: i) a capital recovery plan and ii) a liquidity recovery plan. Once the bank moved into resolution, it would be for the supervisory authorities to decide the appropriate strategy on the basis of the resolution plan. The latter would explain the relationships between the different entities within the group and contingency responses in case of interruption of those relationships. The resolution plan will also be required to offer a detailed assessment of the potential obstacles to the use of resolution tools by the authorities. The bank will also need to identify the market and payment infrastructures to which they are connected and plan to disconnect itself from those systems in an orderly manner (FSA, 2009b).

to have a clear and comprehensive picture of banks activities and for resolution authorities to disentangle functions in case of crisis and failure.

As has been mentioned (Box 3.1), the Basel working group on cross-border bank resolution (BCBS, 2009b) has suggested that full consolidation could be accompanied by partial ring-fencing to protect systemically significant functions in a crisis, but not the financial institution itself, with positive effects on market resiliency and confidence. However, extending this approach to subsidiaries and, as some have suggested, even branches of foreign banks in the host jurisdiction, would utterly undermine the universal solution, and should be rejected.

4. NEW SUPERVISORY ARRANGEMENTS AT EU LEVEL

The financial crisis has confirmed that there is neither an optimal nor a superior financial supervisory structure. A wave of reform of supervisory models has swept through many countries in the last 20 years, either leading to a 'single regulator' model or to a regulatory architecture by objective.

These reforms were justified by the blurring of boundaries between intermediaries, which undermined the traditional regulation by sector of activities (banking, securities, insurance)[73] – in spite of some important persisting differences across sectors (Half & Jackson, 2002). At all events, no supervisory structure emerged as a clear winner in confronting the crisis; in the United Kingdom, coordination failures between the FSA and the Bank of England played a role in scaring Northern Rock depositors.

As was to be expected, regulatory and supervisory arrangements mainly organised along national lines proved especially inadequate in tackling the cross-border dimensions of regulation and supervision. Within the European Union the crisis has exposed large loopholes in the allocation of supervisory tasks and the absence of rules for burden-sharing in case of crisis of a large EU cross-border banking group. It has become all too clear that cross-border banking, while bringing remarkable benefits, also poses formidable challenges for financial stability.

Indeed, the EU authorities have been confronted with the 'trilemma' on how to reconcile the three objectives of financial stability, national

---

[73] See De Luna Martinez & Rose (2003).

supervision and integrated financial markets.[74] Only two of the three objectives may be achieved at the same time: with integrated financial markets financial stability requires at least some centralisation of supervisory powers for crisis prevention and crisis management at the EU level. However, not only have supervisory powers on large cross-border EU banking groups not been centralised at the EU level, but the allocation of tasks between home and host country authorities has created significant fragmentation in oversight.

A key principle introduced by the Second Banking Directive is home country control. In compliance with this principle, the Capital Requirements Directive (CRD, 2006/48/EC) assigns responsibility for the consolidated supervision of 'credit institutions', including branches and subsidiaries, to the home country authority; host country authorities supervise 'on a solo basis' locally incorporated subsidiaries and have limited oversight of branches (regarding liquidity, see Article 41 of the CRD).[75] Supervisory arrangements mirror the allocation of tasks between the home and host country regarding deposit guarantee and winding up and reorganisation of credit institutions (see Table 4.1).

The architecture of supervision follows the legal structure of banking groups; however, Article 131 of the CRD provides that the host-country authority may choose to delegate its responsibility for the supervision of subsidiaries to the home-country authority. When the host-country supervisor delegates supervision, then the home-country supervisor has exclusive oversight over the entire group, both on consolidated and solo basis (Garcia et al., 2009). Delegation has the great merit of permitting fully consolidated supervision, but encounters formidable challenges due to the

---

[74] On the trilemma of financial stability, see Schoenmaker (2009).

[75] However, Article 42a of the Capital Requirements Directive 2006/48/EC, inserted by Directive 2009/111/EC, has strengthened coordination and information-sharing mechanisms between the home and host authorities of systemically significant branches: host country authorities may request to the home country authority that a branch of a credit institution be considered significant on the basis of the deposit share of the branch in the host country (if higher than 2%); the impact of closure or suspension of operation of the branch on market liquidity and the payment, clearing and settlement systems in the host country; the size and the importance of the branch in terms of the number of clients within the banking or financial system of the host country.

conflicts of interest between the home and host authorities, as will be described.

Table 4.1 Allocation to home and host country of supervision, deposit insurance and resolution functions in the European Union

	Prudential Supervisor	Deposit insurance regulators	Reorganisation and winding up authority
Banks locally incorporated			
Parent banks authorised in home country	Home country authorising parent bank (consolidated supervision – solvency)	Home country	Home country
Subsidiaries of parent banks headquartered in another EU country	Home country authorising parent bank (consolidated supervision – solvency) Host country authorising the subsidiary ('solo' basis)	Host country	Host country*
Branches Branches of banks headquartered in another EU country	Home country of head office (consolidated supervision – solvency) Host country (liquidity)	Home country (possibility of supplementing the guarantee by host country)	Home country

*While this is the formal legal arrangement, in practice the home country will also intervene in view of its responsibility for consolidated supervision.

Source: Mayes et al. (2007).

The current structure of EU cross-border supervision entails a misalignment in incentives between home- and host-country supervisors when dealing with a faltering financial institution (Eisenbeis & Kaufman, 2006; Herring, 2007). In particular, host countries are exposed to the impact of a crisis of local entities of foreign banks without adequate instruments of defence, in regard of both locally incorporated subsidiaries and local branches (which do not even have a separate balance sheet and income statement, being included in the parent company's accounts). The vulnerability of host countries may be higher with regard to branches, since the host supervisor is unable to ascertain the real situation of the parent bank; the Icelandic crisis has shown vividly that the presumption of support by the parent company in case of need may be illusory.

Home/host conflicts are exacerbated by asymmetries in financial resources and human capital of supervisors, the financial and legal infrastructure, and above all risk exposures (Herring, 2007). Risk exposure for the host country is higher when the foreign subsidiaries is large within the country, but relatively small or functionally unimportant for the parent bank and the home country, as is typically the case in small countries with a strong presence of foreign banks. The agency problem is exacerbated by cross-border banking groups typically centralising key corporate functions (e.g. liquidity, IT, large corporate lending, etc.) – which is not an accident but a main source of competitive advantage related to size and globalised operations.

In case of crisis of a cross-border banking group, this structure of incentives entails strong home-country bias by national supervisors, which will give priority to national interests with little regard for repercussions in the host country. Home-country bias may also entail the promotion of national champions internationally (Eisenbeis & Kaufman, 2006), so that oversight of foreign operations tends to become more lenient. This may lead in turn to the parent bank undertaking excessive risks in its foreign operations with little effective oversight both by the home and the host authority. Competition within the EU market would also be distorted.

The division of labour in the supervision of cross-border groups is strictly related to the fiscal responsibility for losses generated by bank failures. Lack of burden-sharing arrangements is a crucial factor exacerbating the agency problem between home and host country authorities; without clear commitments each country will tend to follow a beggar-my-neighbour policy. For instance, in the Fortis crisis the memorandum of understanding (MoU) between the supervisory authorities was swept aside as soon as the bank's survival came into question, precisely because there was no agreement on burden-sharing. While the Belgian authorities were separately negotiating the sale of the bank's main assets to a French banking group, the Dutch authorities did not hesitate to seize all banking and insurance assets within their jurisdiction and break up the group.

4.1 Commission proposals for a new EU supervisory structure[76]

The new supervisory structure proposed by the European Commission, now under consideration by Council and Parliament, may have a strong bearing on bank resolution regimes in the EU, although they do not modify national bankruptcy systems *strictu sensu*.

On top of the new structure will be the European Systemic Risk Board (ESRB), which will give general risk warnings and recommendations on specific risks. It will specify the procedures to be followed by the European Supervisory Authorities (ESAs) – part in turn of the European System of Financial Supervisors (ESFS) – to act upon its recommendations. The ESAs from their side should use their powers to ensure the timely follow-up to recommendations addressed to one or more competent national supervisory authorities.

All new legislative measures are regulations, hence they will be directly applicable, with no need of transposition into national law. A political agreement on the different measures was reached in the EU Council in December 2009 under the Swedish presidency. The EU Parliament is currently considering the proposals but intends to go much further.

The ESRB will only be consultative but will supposedly derive its authority from its reputation and expertise. It will be run by the ECB and be largely composed of EU central bankers, with limited participation of supervisors, and one representative of the Economic and Financial Committee. The ESAs, on the other hand, will have legal personality, with power to impose binding agreements to effectively coordinate supervision of cross-border groups, and will be composed of national regulators and supervisors. An important limitation in its powers, however, is that such

---

[76] This section was prepared by Karel Lannoo.

decisions could not impinge upon the fiscal responsibilities of the member states, hence the powers to liquidate a bank would remain at the home country level, in cooperation with the respective host countries.

The changes which are being discussed in the United States (House Wall Street Act of 11 December 2009) are different from the EU since they assign macro-prudential oversight mainly to the Secretary of the Treasury, who will chair the Financial Services Oversight Council (FSOC), bringing together the different supervisory authorities and the Federal Reserve. The chair of the FSOC could make a systemic risk determination with respect to a specific financial company, and could order that it be placed under resolution. Excess dissolution costs would be paid by a Systemic Dissolution Fund (SDF) run by the Federal Deposit Insurance Corporation (FDIC).[77]

The role of the ESRB. The ESRB will be at the centre of the new EU oversight system, even if this body will only be consultative. Its twelve-member Steering Committee is composed of the seven ESCB members (including the President of the ECB), the three chairs of the European Supervisory Authorities, a member of the EU Commission and the President of the Economic and Financial Committee (EFC). The dominance of the central bankers in the governance of the new structure is even clearer in the General Board of the ESRB, which comprises, apart from the Steering Committee members, all central bank governors of the EU-27.

The ESRB will have its seat in the ECB and will rely on the analytical and administrative services and skills of this well-reputed and established institution. Thus, de facto it will be controlled by the ECB. The Finance Ministers have only one representative in the ESRB. Hence, notwithstanding the declaration of the Finance Ministers that they want to be in the driver's seat, the power on top of the new EU oversight system will reside with the central bankers.

The ESRB should define, identify and prioritise all macro-financial risks; issue risk warnings and give recommendations to policy-makers, supervisors and eventually to the public; monitor the follow-up of the risk warnings, and warn the EU Council in the event that the follow-up is found to be inappropriate; liaise with international and third country

---

[77] For a comparison of the EU and US proposed reforms, see Schinasi (2009) and Lannoo (2010).

counterparts; and report at least bi-annually to the EU Council and European Parliament.

The ESRB should have access to all micro-prudential data and indicators. It could request the ESAs to provide information in summary or collective form. Should this information be unavailable (or not made available), the ESRB will have the possibility to request data directly from national supervisory authorities, national central banks or other authorities of member states.

Crisis management is not mentioned as a task of the ESRB, but of the ESFS. This is a departure from the ad hoc agreement reached in the European Council in October 2008, whereby the President of the ECB (in conjunction with the other European central banks) formed part of a financial crisis cell, with the President of the Commission, the EU Council and the Eurogroup. The question thus remains to what extent the ESRB will be involved in micro-prudential matters. Would it, as the US Financial Services Oversight Council, be involved in recommending that a specific financial company poses a systemic risk, and order it to be broken up? This seems unlikely for the time being, given the sensitivity of member states with regard to fiscal powers, but is something that will need to be addressed sooner rather than later.

The role of the EBA. Under the proposed Regulation 2009/0142, the European Banking Authority will replace the Committee of European Banking Supervisors (CEBS), with a modified statutory role and broader powers in regulation and supervision at EU level, with also affects bank crisis resolution.

The EBA will be responsible for:

a. moving towards the realisation of a single rulebook and its enforcement, by developing technical implementation standards that will be given legal enforceability throughout the Union by Commission endorsement;

b. ensuring harmonised supervisory practices and peer review of national authorities;

c. strengthening oversight of cross-border groups, including by participating in supervisory colleges (albeit only as 'observer', see Article 12 of the proposed regulation establishing the EBA);

d. coordinating EU-wide stress tests to assess the resilience of financial institutions to adverse market developments;

e.   establishing a central European database aggregating all micro-prudential information; and

f.   ensuring a coordinated response in crisis situations.

The proposed reforms will not modify the current emphasis on home country control but should allow it to function better. The EBA will formally participate in the Colleges of supervisors of cross-border groups, albeit only with observer status – an element of weakness that can yet be corrected; it will have to ensure that Colleges of supervisors effectively function as colleges[78] and that information sharing works and, in case of disagreements, it will have formal powers to mediate between supervisory authorities. It will conduct regular peer reviews of supervisors with the goal of enhancing consistency in supervisory outcomes (Article 15). And under Article 13 of the proposed regulation, it "shall facilitate the delegation of tasks and responsibilities between competent authorities": this provision clearly applies to the delegation of powers for crisis resolution.

In emergency situations, the EBA shall facilitate and coordinate the actions taken by the relevant national supervisory authorities, and may also take decisions requiring national supervisory authorities to take action to remedy an emergency situation (Article 10). The power to determine the existence of an emergency situation will be in the hands of the EU Council, following consultation with the Commission, the ESRB and the ESAs: a cumbersome procedure that may be inconsistent with the rapid decisions required in emergency – the EBA should be allowed to act independently in this regard, we believe. The EBA will also be charged with coordinating EU-wide stress test and, to this end, it will establish a central European database, thus being at the centre of information gathering and dissemination.

Article 10.2 provides that the EBA can call on national authorities to take action to address "adverse developments that may jeopardize the orderly functioning and integrity of financial markets or the stability ... of the financial system"; in case the competent authorities failed to comply, the Commission proposal had also envisaged, under Article 10.3, that the

---

[78] Begg (2009) offers an in-depth review of the pros and cons of the college approach. On the functioning of Colleges, on the whole, he is fairly critical of present arrangements.

EBA could directly address an individual decision to a financial institution "requiring the necessary action to comply with its obligations ... including the cessation of any practice". These powers would be essential in resolving banking crises, but were eliminated in the ECOFIN compromise of December 3, 2009. In its draft report, the competent European Parliament Committee has restored the Commission text and has strengthened the role of the EBA, allowing it to appeal before national courts against decisions taken by national authorities.

The creation of the ESRB and the ESAs are a big step forward towards a more unified European regulatory and supervisory system, also for bank resolution regimes. However, many questions remain unresolved and can only gradually find an answer, as the new structures emerge. The biggest problem ahead will be to find a proper balance between the new European entities and the home and host country powers and structures. Some further steps forward feasible within the present Treaty structure are outlined below.

4.2 Supervisory powers for resolution of pan-European banks

Following the recent crisis, many countries advocated full ring-fencing of financial organisations operating within any given jurisdiction, which would then be subject to host authorities' full regulatory and supervisory powers in banking crisis resolution, as the only practicable solution. Host country powers would notably include the possibility to ring-fence the assets of branches and subsidiaries, or the option for the host country to impose the establishment of locally incorporated subsidiaries with own capital and liquidity, and adequately separate operating functions ('subsidiarisation')[79] – something that runs up against freedom of establishment but in practice has been happening already in jurisdictions with a large presence of foreign banks, e.g. in Eastern Europe.

---

[79] Strauss-Kahn argued that since "major banks manage their funding and lending risks globally ... [if they] ... have to lock up pools of liquidity in every national jurisdiction, their capacity for intermediating capital across borders could fall, and their charges for doing so rise, to the detriment of the world economy" (Dominique Strauss-Kahn, "Nations must think globally on finance reform", *Financial Times*, 18 February 2010).

This approach has started to look attractive also to the authorities in the main financial centres, most notably the UK Financial Services Authority (FSA, 2009a) on grounds that this is the only solution in the absence of a complete EU framework. However, this approach obviously entails significant efficiency losses of reduced integration of banking and would damage the EU single market.

A viable alternative would be to maintain the current allocation of powers between home and host authorities, but concentrate certain supervisory powers at EU level, building upon the Commission proposals that have been described.

Strengthened obligations to cooperate at EU level in information sharing are already contained in the revised CRD (see Directive 2009/111/EC) and the proposed regulation for the establishment of the EBA. The revised CRD requires that the consolidating supervisor shall establish Colleges of supervisors to facilitate the exercise of powers in Articles 129 (information gathering and dissemination, and also planning and coordination of supervisory activities "in preparation for and during emergency situations") and 131 (delegation and written coordination and cooperation agreements), under guidelines for the operation of Colleges that will be issued by the EBA.[80]

However, these coordination arrangements still seem to fall short of what is needed in case of crisis of a cross-border group, as was vividly shown by the fate of MoUs when crisis struck pan-European groups like Fortis. The key weakness in MoUs is that they do not provide host countries with strong and credible guarantees that their national interests and stakeholders will be treated fairly by the home country authorities, and that domestic financial stability will not be compromised by decisions taken abroad which they would be unable to influence.

Indeed, what is needed is arrangements that will make it possible to exploit the benefits of fully consolidated ('universal') supervision and resolution by the parent company's authorities and at the same time

---

[80] While the establishment of Colleges is compulsory, their decisions are not binding. The Omnibus Directive (2009/0161), proposed by the Commission in October 2009, amends Article 131a(2) to provide that EBA shall develop draft technical standards for the operational functioning of Colleges, and submit those draft technical standards to the Commission by 1 January 2014.

reassure host country authorities that their interests are fully and fairly taken into account, so that delegation of powers to the home country authority becomes acceptable. Otherwise, consolidation and delegation would not be acceptable: for the simple reason that the home country supervisor would be responsible for financial stability in the host country without being accountable to the host country government and taxpayers (Eisenbeis & Kaufman, 2006).

What is needed is an integrated system of supervision, deposit guarantee, crisis management and resolution capable of providing the host country with adequate protection and participation in the 'universal' consolidated supervision and resolution procedure. This system has three procedural building blocks: a new EU Deposit Guarantee Agency (EDGA) handling deposit guarantee for cross-border banking groups; a private contract between EDGA and guaranteed banking groups specifying their commitments and obligations on disclosure and living wills; an EU system of mandated corrective action for cross-border banking groups in difficulty effectively banning supervisory forbearance.

4.3   A new framework for supervision

The new European System of Financial Supervisors envisages a network of national and EU supervisory authorities, leaving supervision of financial institutions at the national level and entrusting coordination of cross-border groups to strengthened Colleges of supervisors led by the parent banks' home authorities. This solution is inadequate because it leaves ample supervisory gaps and room for conflict between national supervisors, and thus great uncertainty as to who is responsible for doing what. A step forward is needed.

All pan-European banking groups should be supervised, subject to mandated corrective action and resolved on a consolidated basis under the law of the parent company. The universal principle should cover foreign branches and subsidiaries – with the sole exception of subsidiaries that could demonstrably survive as stand-alone entities even in case of dissolution of the parent company.

Under this new EU framework, supervision, mandated corrective action and resolution would still be managed by the strengthened Colleges of supervisors, under the leadership of the parent company supervisor: but it would the responsibility of the EBA to supervise the procedure, sanction all key decisions, resolve disputes, and ensure fair treatment of all interested parties. Colleges would bring all of their proposals to the EBA, which would give them legal power with its own decisions: including the start of mandated corrective action and forced recapitalisation, changes in management, selling assets, branches and segments of activity, or set up a bridge bank, and the resolution of disputes that may arise between national supervisors and individual stakeholders.

In this manner the benefits of using existing supervisory structures would be combined with the elimination of distorted incentives and conflicts of interests between national supervisors. Placing the EBA at the centre of the system of universal resolution thus is critical for its acceptance: this is the crucial step in order to sell centralised universal resolution to all stakeholders.

The proposed Omnibus Directive (2009/0161) already envisages that the consolidating supervisor shall inform the EBA of the activities of the Colleges of supervisors, including in emergency situations, and communicate all the information of particular relevance for the purposes of supervisory convergence. At all events, it seems also appropriate to have in the Colleges a full member designated by the EBA, as has been mentioned.

This new supervisory structure should have full power to manage mandated action and resolution of cross-border banking groups on a consolidated basis (Chapter 3). A new European Deposit Guarantee Agency should be set up as an EBA arm entrusted with the management of a new European Deposit Guarantee Fund, based on the principles and rules outlined in Chapter 2. Protection of depositors at national banks with no significant cross-border activities could remain with national systems, which of course would need much less funds than today.

All European deposit-taking financial institutions with significant cross-border deposits basis would be required to join the EU deposit guarantee scheme and, in order to do so, would be required to sign a contract with EDGA committing them to provide supervisors and the EBA with full information on group organisation, functional lines and counterparties – including 'living wills' detailing how the various creditors and stakeholders would be treated in case of failure (see Chapter 3).

4.4   A European system of Mandated Corrective Action

As has been argued, a system of mandated corrective action by supervisors acting early as banks under their surveillance show emerging signs of undercapitalisation and funding difficulties, is key to contain moral hazard created by the deposit guarantee and protect the guarantee fund. Mandated early action is also of the essence to inhibit regulatory forbearance.

The key issue is one of incentives. Benston & Kaufman (1988) argued that the introduction of a system of Structured Early Intervention and Resolution (SEIR) is necessary in order to make deposit insurance incentive compatible. Their model is based on capital thresholds, so that as capital ratios decline the regulator is allowed or obliged to impose corrective measures, which become progressively more pervasive with falling capital ratios. Reorganisation and liquidation are mandatory when capital falls below critical thresholds.

This was the model introduced in the United States for depository banks in 1991 with the Federal Deposit Insurance Corporation Improvement Act: a system of Prompt Corrective Action (PCA) for insured depository institutions was created to "resolve the problems of insured depository institutions at the least possible long-term loss to the Deposit Insurance Fund".[81] As shown in Table 4.2, the PCA system introduced five 'capital zones' for insured depository institutions: well capitalised, adequately capitalised, undercapitalised, significantly undercapitalised and critically undercapitalised. The capitalisation ratios are calculated both on risk-adjusted and unadjusted basis. Corrective measures are in part compulsory, in part left to the authorities' discretion, and include a broad range of requirements and restrictions (e.g. suspension of dividend payments, restriction of asset growth, compulsory recapitalisation). When a bank is critically undercapitalised, authorities are obliged to close it, and this happens well before capital is depleted.

---

[81] US Code, Title 12, Chapter 16, Section 1831o, Prompt corrective action, (a)(1).

Table 4.2 Summary of Prompt Corrective Action Provisions of the Federal Deposit Insurance Corporation Improvement Act of 1991

Zone	Mandatory Provisions	Discretionary Provisions	Capital Ratios (percent) Risk Based Total	Risk Based Tier 1	Leverage Tier 1
1. Well capitalized			>10	>6	>5
2. Adequately capitalized	1. No brokered deposits, except with FDIC approval		>8	>4	>4
3. Undercapitalized	1. Suspend dividends and management fees 2. Require capital restoration plan 3. Restrict asset growth 4. Approval required for acquisitions, branching, and new activities 5. No brokered deposits	1. Order recapitalization 2. Restrict inter-affiliate transactions 3. Restrict deposit interest rates 4. Restrict certain other activities 5. Any other action that would better carry out prompt corrective action	<8	<4	<4
4. Significantly undercapitalized	1. Same as for Zone 3 2. Order recapitalization* 3. Restrict inter-affiliate transactions* 4. Restrict deposit interest rates* 5. Pay of officers restricted	1. Any Zone 3 discretionary actions 2. Conservatorship or receivership if fails to submit or implement plan or recapitalize pursuant to order 3. Any other Zone 5 provision, if such action is necessary to carry out prompt corrective action	<6	<3	<3
5. Critically undercapitalized	1. Same as for Zone 4 2. Receiver/conservator within 90 days* 3. Receiver if still in Zone 5 four quarters after becoming critically under-capitalized 4. Suspend payments on subordinated debt* 5. Restrict certain other activities				<2

* Not required if primary supervisor determines action would not serve purpose of prompt corrective action or if certain other conditions are met.

Source: Eisenbeis & Kaufman (2006).

Following the US example, under the deposit guarantee system that we have outlined, the EBA should have full powers, and indeed be obliged to act to impose changes in management, recapitalisation and asset disposals of cross-border banks as capital falls.[82] Action must start well before net worth becomes negative, based on predetermined automatic triggers. It should be stressed that without mandated corrective action, rather than purging the system from moral hazard, the deposit guarantee will inevitably end up rescuing failing deposit-taking institutions, the fund will be rapidly depleted and taxpayers will be called in to foot the bill. There should be no doubts that the system of mandated corrective action is there to ensure the protection of the guarantee fund, not financial institutions.

A European system of Mandated Corrective Action (EMCA) must have three features.[83] First, in the United States PCA is based on uniformly defined capital and leverage ratios, based on US rules, so that no problem of geographic inconsistency arises. Conversely, the definition of capital across European countries is heterogeneous, due to the discretion left by the Capital Requirements Directive in national implementation. However, for the EMCA system to work properly, the definition of capital (total capital and Tier 1 capital) should be the same across European countries, to avoid geographic distortions and regulatory arbitrage. There is also a need to agree on uniform application of accounting principles for all pan-European groups, including those operating also in the United States with subsidiaries that may use US GAAP rather than the IFRS (see Box 4.1).

EBA, which is already charged with harmonising supervisory tools and practices, should also be entrusted with the task of standardising the triggers for early intervention. This implies an enormous workload, as even for quantitative measures, such as non-performing loans, no harmonised

---

[82] Unicredit Group (2009) proposed that EBA be empowered with the authority to nominate a task force for corrective action. The task force would have the objective of preventing nationally-based discrimination and ring-fencing; it would collect information, review management decisions and coordinate private solutions, regarding the group as a single entity and taking into account all possible externalities.

[83] For a proposal to introduce a system of corrective action in Europe see ESFRC (1998) and ESFRC (2005). Mayes et al. (2007) and Nieto & Wall (2006) analysed the preconditions and the desirability of a PCA system in Europe.

measurement exists in the EU at present. And it is even more difficult for qualitative measures, e.g. when and how to replace (parts of) the management or the board of a bank, sell businesses or create a bridge bank.

Second, in the US system intervention thresholds include reference to an absolute leverage ratio, while in the European Union leverage for regulatory purposes is calculated on a risk-adjusted basis. As we have argued, in practice risk-adjusted capital requirements are not only easy to circumvent but also logically flawed, since risk cannot be measured independently of market sentiment, and therefore should be scrapped altogether. Be that as it may, for the purposes of early mandated action reference to absolute leverage is a must, as the only unquestionable indicator of capital strength not open to interpretation (at least to the extent that the accounting definition of capital is unambiguous).

The third requirement for an effective EMCA is that it should apply to deposit-taking banking groups at a consolidated level. The application of EMCA at the consolidated level is key to tackle the implicit guarantee for deposit-taking of which the entire group benefits and should aim at avoiding the concentration of excessive leverage in non-depository subsidiaries. The US prompt corrective action, for example, is an incomplete system, as highlighted by the financial crisis: in fact, it applies only to depository institutions and not to banking groups as a whole. As a result, the high leverage of the major bank holding companies was concentrated outside of their major deposit-taking subsidiaries: the lack of corrective action powers for non-depository financial institutions and for bank holding companies impeded the prompt intervention by the FDIC and other federal supervisors.[84]

Box 4.1 What is in a leverage ratio?

The leverage ratio (capital/total assets) should show the maximum (percentage) loss a bank can make on its assets before losing all of its capital. It has thus been proposed to add a crude leverage ratio to the standard risk weighted capital ratios under the Basel regime. However, this idea raises one practical and conceptual problem: a transatlantic comparison of leverage

---

[84] The US financial reform currently being examined by the Congress envisages the extension of prompt corrective action to systemically important financial institutions.

ratios is almost impossible given the different accounting principles used in the EU (IFRS) and the US (GAAP).

The key problem is that these two accounting systems yield in general similar results, but they present completely different pictures in the case of derivatives. Derivative exposure is reported gross under IFRS, but net under US GAAP. The case of Deutsche Bank shows what difference this can make. Under IFRS Deutsche Bank has a balance sheet (as measured by assets) of around €2 trillion. Deutsche Bank has published its own evaluation of how large its balance would be under US GAAP, arriving at only €1 trillion. Assuming Deutsche Bank knows how to apply US GAAP, this implies that its leverage would be halved if it were judged under US GAAP.

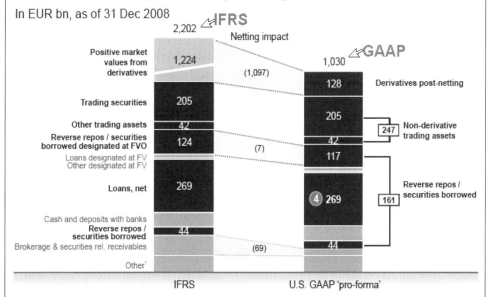

Total assets: Analysis of major categories

Source: Ackermann (2009b).

The key difference between IFRS and US GAAP is thus the treatment of the item called (under IFRS) 'Positive market values from derivatives', equal to €1.224 billion on Deutsche Bank's IFRS balance sheet. Under US GAAP this item would shrink to about one tenth, with only 128 billion appearing under 'derivatives post netting'. A similar observation applies to the liability side of the balance sheet. Under IFRS Deutsche Bank shows also over 1.2 in liabilities under 'market values of derivatives', which presumably would also be reduced by a factor of about 10 under US GAAP.*

What is the reason for this huge difference in the way derivatives show up in the balance sheet? Here is an explanation from an accounting point of view: "IAS 39 Financial instruments is the core standard under IFRS for derivatives. It is a complex and somewhat controversial accounting standard that has been the subject of extensive debate. Essentially IAS 39 is based on a simple premise – derivatives must be recognized on the balance sheet at fair value. Historically, under many national GAAP, driven by a historical cost perspective, derivatives remained unrecognised as there is no initial cost, as in a swap, for example. The only recognition of their effect may be the matching of the relevant underlying with the derivative on settlement. Therefore a company could have an entire portfolio of derivatives at the year end with little or no recognition in the financials as there is no upfront cost as such."** This passage suggests that under US GAAP most derivatives do not appear on balance sheets as there is no initial cost.

This difference between IFRS and US GAAP could resolve to some extent the mystery why the US authorities were surprised by the extent of the market reaction to Lehman: Lehman's balance sheet reflected US GAAP and thus did not show the extent of the exposure of other market participants. It is likely that the balance sheet of Lehman under IFRS would have been several times larger, thus giving a better picture of the importance of Lehman. An IFRS balance for Lehman would have given a better picture of the importance of this operator for the market.

Moreover, a balance sheet under IFRS would give a better picture of the exposure of the bank itself to counterparty risk. Assume a bank has a large amount of derivatives contracts outstanding, but without any net exposure. It could still make very large losses in case important counterparties fail.

---

* For other categories (loans, repos, etc.) the difference between IFRS and US GAAP are minor. This implies that transatlantic comparisons should still be possible for banks without a large derivatives exposure. However, this is not the case for investment banks (or the investment banking arms of EU universal banks). And in this crisis the problems arose often in the investment banking side.

** Source: http://accounting-financial-tax.com/2009/04/accounting-treatment-for-derivatives-gaap-under-ifrs/. In the US unlisted investments available for sale are stated at cost whereas under IFRS they are recorded at fair value once a reasonably reliable measure can be established.

Source: Gros (2010).

4.5 Burden-sharing arrangements

As has been described, the key problem with existing nation-based arrangements is that they do not incorporate the cross-border externalities that may be generated by the failure of a pan-European bank: hence, the authorities in the home country charged with the consolidated supervision of EU banking groups tend to disregard the negative spillovers that might occur in host countries from the crisis of the group or local subsidiaries. The resulting coordination failure in crisis management and resolution is aggravated by a lack of ex-ante agreements for sharing the costs of liquidation across countries, in case of bankruptcy of a cross-border financial group. Experience has confirmed over and over again that supervisory cooperation can hardly survive when a crisis occurs and losses have to be divided; in the absence of ex-ante burden-sharing criteria, beggar-thy-neighbour policies may prevail and make crisis management and resolution more complex and costly (Herring, 2007).

This issue cannot be resolved here and is only examined cursorily for the sake of completeness. The system of deposit guarantee cum early mandated action that we have outlined goes a long way towards reducing the eventual burden for taxpayers of a banking crisis, but it cannot eliminate it altogether.

Therefore, it might be advisable to create a last line of defence through the creation of a fund for the liquidation of emerging losses from a banking crisis that cannot possibly be borne by creditors and shareholders; ideally, such fund should be privately financed, i.e. by the financial system itself. Proposals for such a 'resolution fund' have been put forth recently by authoritative spokesmen for the banking system. However, these proposals have one fundamental weakness: since banks have declared their unwillingness to finance it ex-ante, and propose that funds be raised from capital markets, a public guarantee will inevitably be required to convince investors to buy those securities. Therefore, the possibility of an eventual fallout onto taxpayers still looms large.

An alternative would be to create a straight public fund. Goodhart & Shoenmaker (2009) have proposed the creation of a 'general fund' to be managed by the ECB[85] or by the European Investment Bank, entrusted with the recapitalisation of large EU banks in case of crisis. This fund is an

---

[85] See also Goodhart & Shoenmaker (2006).

example of 'generic' burden-sharing by countries proportionate to the size of the participating countries: the burden is apportioned between countries, regardless of the location of the failing bank. Alternatively, a 'specific' burden-sharing might be envisaged, whereby only countries in which distressed banks are present should bear the cost of support. Along these lines, a proposal for a European Financial Protection Fund has been put forth by the Rapporteur of the Economic and Financial Committee of the European Parliament, Garcia-Margallo, in his draft report on the regulation establishing the EBA (see his proposed Article 12a). The fund aims at protecting European depositors and reduces the cost for taxpayers of a systemic financial crisis; it would be financed by European financial institutions and by issuance of debt guaranteed by the member states. In exceptional circumstances and in a systemic crisis, should these resources be insufficient, the affected member states would bear the cost according to burden-sharing arrangements based on a combination of criteria, including assets, deposits, revenues and share of the payment system.

Overall, in any burden-sharing model the key problem is the objective determination of the costs falling on each country: a mix of complementary indicators might be identified by the EU Council based for instance on the size and geographical distribution of banking assets and liabilities, and perhaps other factors such as income and employees.

As already mentioned, however, the circumstances when the fund would be authorised to intervene must be carefully circumscribed, since otherwise moral hazard would re-enter the system from the back door and market discipline would be weakened once again. Intervention by the fund should only be permitted as a last resort, to cover liquidation losses for clear public-interest reasons, and never for shareholders. At all events, a key obstacle related to ex-ante burden-sharing with public resources is that parliaments in the member states would in all likelihood resist the idea of setting aside resources in national budgets to bail out private firms.

Perhaps, the only viable solution, entailing minimum distortions to private incentives, would be for the member states to decide a key for allocating residual losses between themselves, and rely on the EBA and supervisory mechanisms that have been described to minimise any such residual losses. The key would also apply in case a new systemic crisis called again for massive government interventions.

REFERENCES

Acharya, V. (2009), "Systemic risk and deposit insurance premiums", VoxEU, 4 September (http://www.voxeu.org/index.php?q=node/3941).

Acharya, V., T. Cooley, M. Richardson and I. Walter (2009), *Real time solutions for US financial reform*, Stern Working Group on Financial Reform, NYU, December.

Acharya, V., J.A.C. Santos and T. Yorulmazer (2009), "Systemic Risk and Deposit Insurance Premiums", *Economic Policy Review*, Federal Reserve Bank of New York.

Ackermann, J. (2009a), "Statement at the Deutsche Bank Reception", Brussels, 17 November.

———— (2009b), "Financial Transparency", presentation at Roadshow in Montreal and Toronto, 19-20 February (http://www.deutsche-bank.de/ir/en/download/Roadshow_Canada_Ackermann_19_-_20_Feb.pdf).

Alessandri, P. and A.G. Haldane (2009), *Banking on the State*, Bank of England, November.

ABI (Associazione Bancaria Italiana) (2010), *The ABI response to the Commission's Communication "an EU cross-border crisis management framework in the banking sector"- Consultation's questions*, 20 January.

Avgouleas, E., C.A.E. Goodhart and D. Schoenmaker (2010), *Living Wills as a Catalyst for Action*, Wharton Financial Institutions Center, Working Paper 10-09, Wharton School, University of Pennsylvania, Philadelphia.

Bank of England (2007), *Financial Stability Report,* No. 22, October.

Barth, J.R., G. Caprio and R.E. Levine (2008), *Database on Bank Regulation and Supervision*, updated June 2008 (http://econ.worldbank.org).

Baxter, T.C. (2010), *Factors Affecting Efforts to Limit Payments to AIG Counterparties*, Testimony before the Committee on Government Oversight and Reform, U.S. House of Representatives, 27 January (http://www.newyorkfed.org/newsevents/speeches/2010/bax100127.html).

BCBS (Basel Committee on Banking Supervision) (2009a), *Strengthening the resilience of the banking sector*, Bank for International Settlements, Basel, December.

_____ (2009b), *Report and Recommendations of the Cross-border Bank Resolution Group*, Bank for International Settlements, Basel, September.

BCBS and IADI (Basel Committee on Banking Supervision and International Association of Deposit Insurers) (2009), *Core Principles for Effective Deposit Insurance Systems*, June.

Beck, T.H.L. (2004), "The incentive-compatible design of deposit insurance and bank failure resolution – Concepts and country studies", in D.G. Mayes and A. Luiksila (eds), *Who pays for bank insolvency?*, Basingstoke, Hampshire: Palgrave Macmillan.

Begg, I. (2009), "Regulation and Supervision of Financial Intermediaries in the EU", *Journal of Common Market Studies*, Vol. 47, No. 5, November.

Benston, G.J. and G.G. Kaufman (1988), *Risk and Solvency Regulation of Depository Institutions: Past Policies and Current Options*, Monograph Series in Finance and Economics, 1988-1, New York, NY: NYU Press.

_____ (1997), *FDICIA after five years: A review and evaluation*, Working Paper 97-01, Federal Reserve Bank of Chicago.

Bernet, B. and S. Walter (2009), *Design, Structure and Implementation of a Modern Deposit Insurance Scheme*, SUERF Studies 2009/5, Vienna: SUERF.

Bliss, R. and G. Kaufman (2007), "U.S. Corporate and Bank Insolvency Regimes: A Comparison and Evaluation", *Virginia Law & Business Review*, Vol. 2, No. 1.

Borio, C. (2003), *Towards a macroprudential framework for financial supervision and regulation?*, BIS Working Paper No. 128, Bank for International Settlements, Basel, February.

Brierley, P. (2009), *The UK Special Resolution Regime for failing banks in an international context*, Financial Stability Paper 5/2009, Bank of England.

Bruner, R.F. and S.D. Carr (2007), *The Panic of 1907. Lessons learned from the market's perfect storm*, Hoboken, NJ: John Wiley & Sons, Inc..

Brunnermeier, M., A. Crockett, C. Goodhart, A. Persaud and H. Shin (2009), *The fundamental principles of financial regulation*, Geneva report on the World Economy No. 11, ICMB (International Center for Monetary and Banking Studies) and CEPR (Centre for Economic Policy Research), January.

Bryan, L. (1991), "Core Banking", *McKinsey Quarterly*, 1.

Buiter, W.H. and A. Sibert (2008), *The Icelandic banking crisis and what to do about it: The lender of last resort theory of optimal currency areas*, Policy Insight No. 26, Centre for Economic Policy Research, October.

Calomiris, C.W. (2000), *U.S. bank deregulation in historical perspective*, Cambridge: Cambridge University Press.

Calomiris, C.W., D. Klingebiel and L. Laeven (2005), "Financial Crisis Policies and Resolution Mechanisms: A Taxonomy from Cross-Country Experience", in P. Honohan and L. Laeven (eds), *Systemic financial crises – containment and resolution*, Cambridge: Cambridge University Press.

Carmassi, J., D. Gros and S. Micossi (2009), "The Global Financial Crisis: Causes and Cures", *Journal of Common Market Studies*, Vol. 47, No. 5, November.

Cerutti, E., G. Dell'Ariccia and M.S. Martínez Pería (2005), *How Banks Go Abroad: Branches or Subsidiaries?*, World Bank Policy Research Working Paper 3753, October.

Chancellor, E. (1999), *Devil Take the Hindmost: A History of Financial Speculation*, London: Macmillan.

Čihák, M. and E. Nier (2009), *The Need for Special Resolution Regimes for Financial Institutions: The Case of the European Union*, IMF Working Paper 09/200, International Monetary Fund, Washington, D.C.

de Larosière Group (2009), *Report by the High-Level Group on Financial Supervision in the European Union*, 25 February.

de Luna Martínez, J. and T.G. Rose (2003), *International Survey of Integrated Financial Sector Supervision*, World Bank Policy Research Working Paper No. 3096n World Bank, Washington, DC.

Demirgüç-Kunt, A. and E. Detragiache (2002), "Does deposit insurance increase banking system stability? An empirical investigation", *Journal of Monetary Economics*, Elsevier, Vol. 49(7), October.

Dermine, J. (2006), "European Banking Integration: Don't Put the Cart Before the Horse," *Financial Markets, Institutions, and Instruments*, Vol. 15, No. 2 May.

Di Noia, C. (1994), *Structuring Deposit Insurance in Europe: Some Considerations and a Regulatory Game*, Wharton Financial Institutions Center, Working Paper 94-31.

Di Noia, C. and S. Micossi, with J. Carmassi and F. Peirce (2009), *Keep It Simple – Policy Responses to the Financial Crisis*, Brussels and Rome: CEPS and Assonime, March.

Eisenbeis, R. and G. Kaufman (2006), *Cross-Border Banking: Challenges for Deposit Insurance and Financial Stability in the European Union*, Working Paper 2006/15, Federal Reserve Bank of Atlanta.

_____ (2009), "Lessons from the Demise of the UK's Northern Rock and the U.S.'s Countrywide and Indymac", in F. Bruni and D.T. Llewellyn (eds), *The Failure of Northern Rock - A Multidimensional Case Study*, SUERF Studies 2009/1, Vienna.

_____ (2010), *Deposit insurance*, in A.N. Berger, P. Molyneux and J. Wilson (eds), *Oxford Handbook of Banking*, Oxford: Oxford University Press.

ESFRC (European Shadow Financial Regulatory Committee) (1998), *Dealing with problem banks in Europe*, Statement No. 1, 22 June.

_____ (2005), *Reforming Banking Supervision in Europe*, Statement No. 23, 21 November.

European Central Bank (2010), *Structural Indicators for the EU banking sector*, January.

European Commission (2009), *An EU Framework for Cross-Border Crisis Management in the Banking Sector*, COM(2009) 561/4, October.

European Commission and International Monetary Fund (2009), "European Commission and IMF welcome reaffirmed commitments of the largest foreign banks in Hungary", IMF press release No. 09/420, 19 November.

FDIC (Federal Deposit Insurance Corporation) (2009), *Quarterly Banking Profile*, Vol. 3, No. 4, Third Quarter.

Freixas, X. (2009), "Monetary Policy in a Systemic Crisis", *Oxford Review of Economic Policy*, forthcoming (http://papers.ssrn.com/sol3/papers.cfm?abstract_id=1503349).

FSA (Financial Services Authority) (2009a), *The Turner Review: A Regulatory Response to the Global Banking Crisis*, London, March.

_____ (2009b), "A regulatory response to the global banking crisis: systemically important banks and assessing the cumulative impact", Turner Review Conference Discussion Paper, October.

FSB (Financial Stability Board) (2009), *Improving Financial Regulation*, Report to G20 Leaders, 25 September.

FSF (Financial Stability Forum) (2009), *FSF Principles for Cross-border Cooperation on Crisis Management*, 2 April.

G-30 (Group of Thirty) (2009), *Financial Reform. A Framework for financial stability*, Report of the Working Group on Financial Reform, Washington, DC, 15 January.

Galbraith, J.K. (1954), *The Great Crash of 1929*, London: Penguin Books.

Garcia, G.G.H., R.M. Lastra and M.J. Nieto (2009), "Bankruptcy and reorganisation procedures for cross-border banks in the EU: Towards an integrated approach to the reform of the EU safety net", *Journal of Financial Regulation and Compliance*, Vol. 17, No. 3, Emerald, Bingley.

Goodhart, C.A.E. and D. Schoenmaker (2006), "Burden Sharing in a Banking Crisis in Europe", *Sveriges Riksbank Economic Review* 2.

Goodhart, C.A.E. and D. Schoenmaker (2009), "Fiscal Burden Sharing in Cross-Border Banking Crises", *International Journal of Central Banking*, Vol. 5, No. 1.

Gorton, G.B. and A. Metrick (2009), *Securitized Banking and the Run on Repo*, Yale ICF Working Paper No. 09-14, November.

Gros, D. (2009), "On the need for a European Deposit Insurance Scheme" (draft, May).

_____ (2010), "Too interconnected to fail = too big to fail: what is in a leverage ratio?", *VoxEU*, 26 January (http://www.voxeu.org/index.php?q=node/4524).

Gros, D. and S. Micossi (2008), "European banking on borrowed time", *Financial Times*, 23 September 2008.

Half, C. and H.E. Jackson (2002), *Background Paper on Evolving Trends in the Supervision of Financial Conglomerates* (http://www.law.harvard.edu/faculty/hjackson/pdfs/2002.Jackson.Half.Evolving.Trends.pdf)

Hardy, D.C. and M.J. Nieto (2008), *Cross-Border Coordination of Prudential Supervision and Deposit Guarantees*, IMF Working Paper 08/283.

Herring, R.J. (2003), "International Financial Conglomerates: Implications for National Insolvency Regimes," in G. Kaufman (ed.), *Market Discipline and Banking: Theory and Evidence*, Amsterdam: Elsevier.

_____ (2007), *Conflicts between Home & Host Country Prudential Supervisors*, Wharton Financial Institutions Center, Working Paper No. 07-33.

Herring, R.J. and J. Carmassi (2010), "The Corporate Structure of International Financial Conglomerates - Complexity and Its Implications for Safety and Soundness", in A.N. Berger, P. Molyneux and J. Wilson (eds), *Oxford Handbook of Banking*, Oxford: Oxford University Press.

Hüpkes, E. (2003), "Insolvency – why a special regime for banks", in *Current Development in monetary and financial law*, Vol. 3, IMF.

_____ (2004), "Too big to save- Toward a functional approach to resolving crises in global financial institutions" in D. Evanoff and G. Kaufman (eds), *Systemic Financial Crises Resolving Large Bank Insolvencies*, World Scientific.

_____ (2009a), "Special bank resolution and shareholders' rights: balancing competing interests", *Journal of Financial Regulation and Compliance*, Vol. 17, No. 3, Emerald, Bingley.

_____ (2009b), "Complicity in complexity: what to do about the 'too-big-to-fail' problem", *Journal of International Banking and Financial Law*, LexisNexis, London, Butterworths, October.

_____ (2009c), "Form follows function" – A new architecture for regulating and resolving global institutions", *European Business Organisation Law Review*, Vol. 10, No. 3, September.

International Association of Deposit Insurers and International Monetary Fund (2009), *Report to the Financial Stability Board on Unwinding Temporary Deposit Insurance Arrangements*, September.

International Monetary Fund (2009), *Global Financial Stability Report*, Washington, D.C., April.

International Monetary Fund and World Bank (2009), *An Overview of the Legal, Institutional, and Regulatory Framework for Bank Insolvency*, April.

JRC (Joint Research Centre, European Commission) (2009), *Possible models for risk-based contributions to EU Deposit Guarantee Schemes*, June.

Kane, E. J. (1989), *The S&Ls Insurance Mess: How Did It Happen?*, Urban Institute Press, Washington, DC.

_____ (1993), "What Lessons Should Japan Learn from the U.S. Deposit-Insurance Mess?", *Journal of the Japanese and International Economies*, 7.

Kaufman, G. (2004), "Depositor liquidity and loss sharing in bank failure resolutions", *Contemporary Economic Policy*, Vol. 22, Wiley-Blackwell.

Kay, J. (2009), *Narrow Banking – The Reform of Banking Regulation, CSFI report*, Centre for the Study of Financial Innovation, London, September.

Kindleberger, C.P. and R. Aliber (2005), *Manias, Panics, and Crashes. A history of financial crises*, Hoboken, NJ: John Wiley & Sons.

King, M. (2009), Speech to Scottish business organisations, Edinburgh, 20 October.

Krimminger, M. (2005), "Banking in a Changing World: Issues and Questions in the Resolution of Cross-Border Banks", paper prepared for Federal Reserve Bank of Chicago Conference on Cross-Border Banking: Regulatory Challenges, 6-7 October.

Laeven, L. and R. Levine (2006), *Is there a Diversification Discount in Financial Conglomerates?*, CEPR Discussion Paper No. 5121, Center for Economic and Policy Research, London, July.

Lannoo, Karel (2010). Comparing the EU and US reponses to the financial crisis, ECMI policy brief 14, January.

Litan, R. (1987), *What Should Banks Do?*, Brookings Institution, Washington, DC.

Llewellyn, D. (2009), "The Northern Rock Crisis: A Multidimensional Problem", in F. Bruni and D.T. Llewellyn (eds), *The Failure of Northern Rock - A Multidimensional Case Study*, SUERF Studies 2009/1, Vienna.

Masera, R. (2009), "Crisis prevention, management and resolution", presentation at the first meeting of the Assonime-CEPS Task Force on Bank Crisis Resolution, 17 July (http://www.ceps.be/taskforce/banking-crisis-resolution-procedures).

Maino, R., R. Masera and G. Mazzoni (2009), *Reform of the Risk Capital Standard (RCS): Towards Basel III*, Milan, draft 16 November.

Mayes, D.G., M.J. Nieto and L. Wall (2007), *Multiple safety net regulators and agency problems in the EU: is Prompt Corrective Action a partial solution?*, Bank of Finland Research Discussion Paper No. 7, Helsinki.

Nieto, M.J. and L. Wall (2006), *Preconditions for a Successful Implementation of Supervisors' Prompt Corrective Action: Is There a Case for a Banking Standard in the European Union?*, Working Paper 2006-27, Federal Reserve Bank of Atlanta, December.

Panzani, L. (2009), "L'insolvenza dei gruppi di società", University of Buenos Aires, II Congreso Internacional de Derecho Comercial y de los Negocios, Buenos Aires, 1-4 June.

Pennacchi (2009), "Deposit insurance", paper prepared for AEI Conference on Private Markets and Public Insurance Programs, March.

Pierce, J. (1991), *The Future of Banking*, New Haven, CT: Yale University Press.

Rochet, J.C. (2008), *Why are there so many banking crises*, Princeton, NJ: Princeton University Press.

Schich, S. (2008), "Financial Crisis: Deposit Insurance and Related Financial Safety Net Aspects", *OECD Journal: Financial Market Trends*, Vol. 2008/2.

_____ (2009), "Expanded Government Guarantees for Bank Liabilities: Selected Issues", *OECD Journal: Financial Market Trends*, Vol. 2009/1.

Schinasi, G. (2009), *More than One Step to Financial Stability*, Bruegel Policy Brief, Issue 2009/06, October.

Schoenmaker, D. (2009), *The Trilemma of Financial Stability* (http://papers.ssrn.com/sol3/papers.cfm?abstract_id=1340395).

Taylor, J. (2009), *Getting Off Track: How Government Actions and Interventions Caused, Prolonged, and Worsened the Financial Crisis*, Stanford, CA: Hoover Institution Press.

Tobin, J. (1958), "Liquidity Preference as Behavior Towards Risk", *Review of Economic Studies*, Vol. 25, No. 2, February.

Tucker, P. (2010), *Shadow banking, capital markets and financial stability*, remarks at a BGC Partners Seminar, London, 21 January.

UNCITRAL (2009), *Practice Guide on Cross-Border Insolvency Cooperation* (http://www.uncitral.org/uncitral/index.html).

Unicredit Group (2009), *Cross-border banking in Europe: What regulation and supervision?*, Discussion Paper No. 1, March.

Volcker, P. (2010), *Statement before the Senate Committee on Banking, Housing and Urban Affairs of the United States*, Hearing on *Prohibiting Certain High-Risk Investment Activities by Banks and Bank Holding Companies*, 2 February.

The White House (2010), *Remarks by the President on Financial Reform*, January 21, available at http://www.whitehouse.gov/the-press-office/remarks-president-financial-reform.

Wolin, N.S. (2010), *Statement before the Senate Committee on Banking, Housing, and Urban Affairs*, Hearing on *Prohibiting Certain High-Risk Investment Activities by Banks and Bank Holding Companies*, 2 February.

Members of the Task Force and Invited Guests and Speakers

Authors: Stefano Micossi   Elisabetta Luchetti
Director General   Legal Expert
Assonime   Assonime

Jacopo Carmassi
Economist
Assonime
Secretary of the Task Force

Contributions by: Daniel Gros   Karel Lannoo
Director   Chief Executive Officer
CEPS   CEPS

Javier Arias Marin   David Bushong
Head European Affairs   Director & Senior Counsellor
BBVA   APCO Worldwide

Rym Ayadi   Alessandra Casale
Senior Research Fellow   Head of Brussels Representative
CEPS   Office
Assonime

Margherita Bianchini
Deputy Director General &   Aurelie Cassou
Head of Corporate Legal Affairs Account Executive
Assonime   Fleishman-Hillard Company

Edward Bowles   Luc Delvaux
Head of Public Affairs, Europe   General Manager
Standard Chartered Bank   BNP Paribas Fortis Bank

Costanza Bufalini   Carmine Di Noia
Head of Institutional Relations Deputy Director General &
with the EU   Head of Capital Markets
UniCredit Group   Assonime

Antonio Hilario Garcia del Riego
Head of Corporate Affairs
in the EU
Banco Santander

Victoria Hardy
Director, Group General
Counsel's Office
Barclays PLC

Anette Hauff
Public Affairs Manager
Deutsche Bank AG

Carl-Christoph Hedrich
Head of Public Affairs
Commerzbank AG

Larisa Ignatova
Counsellor
Mission of Russia to the EU

Nadine Jatto
Consultant
Cabinet DN

Staffan Jerneck
Director &
Director of Corporate Relations
CEPS

Carmine Lamanda
Head of Institutional &
Regulatory Strategic Advisory
Unicredit

Alexandre Lamfalussy
Former President EMI
Institut d'Etudes Européennes

Peter Lindt
Deutsche Bank

Barbara Matthews
Managing Director
BCM International Regulatory
Analytics llc

Donald Ricketts
Head of Financial Services
Fleishman-Hillard Company

Jörn-Jakob Röber
EU Affairs Advisor
Commerzbank Liaison Office
to the EU

Ana Rubio
Chief Economist
BBVA

Jean Saint-Jacques
Minister Counsellor & Deputy
Head of the Mission of Canada
to the EU

Frederik Seeger
Account Executive
Fleishman-Hillard Company

Marek Svoboda
Senior Legal counsel
European Central Bank

Ansgar Tietmeyer
Delegate of the Management
Board for EU Affairs
Deutsche Bank AG

Jouni Timonen
Head of Financial Stability
Central Bank of Finland

Beatrice Vaccari
Deputy Head of Liaison Office
to the EU
UniCredit Group

Freddy Van den Spiegel
Chief Economist,
Director Public Affairs
BNP Paribas Fortis Bank

Katja Würtz
Principal Legal Counsel
ECB

INVITED GUESTS AND SPEAKERS

Erik Bomans
Deminorr

Charles Case
Judge
United States Bankruptcy Court -
District of Arizona

Hans-Joachim Dübel
Finpolconsult

Vitor Gaspar
Banco de Portugal

Eva Hüpkes
Adviser on Regulatory Policy
and Cooperation
Financial Stability Board

Lars Jonung
Research Advisor
DG ECFIN
European Commission

Josina Kamerling
Special Committee
Economic and Social Crisis
European Parliament

Doris Kolassa
Administrator, DG Internal
Market
European Commission

Rosa Lastra
Professor
Queen Mary,
University of London

Sergio Lugaresi
Senior Vice President,
Head of Regulatory Affairs
UniCredit Group

Tobias Mackie
Administrator, DG Internal
Market
European Commission

Rainer Masera
Dean of the Economics Faculty,
Professor of Political Economy,
Member of the Board of the
University of Guglielmo Marconi

Ed Murray
Lawyer
Allen & Overy

Maria Nieto
Advisor
Banco de España

Luciano Panzani
Judge
President of the Court of Turin

Garry Schinasi
International Monetary Fund

Jean-Luc Vallens
Judge/Professor
University of Strasbourg

Ruth Walters
Financial Institutions
European Commission

Georgios S. Zavvos
Legal Advisor - Legal Service
European Commission